THE NEW HEIR'S

GUIDE TO MANAGING

YOUR INHERITANCE

Other Books by Stephen Gadsden
- *The Authoritative Canadian Guide to Understanding Retirement Options* ISBN 0-07-551728-0 $17.99
- *The Canadian Mutual Funds Handbook* ISBN 0-07-552663-8 $18.99
- *The Canadian Guide to Investing for Life* ISBN 0-07-552820-7 $18.99

THE NEW HEIR'S

GUIDE TO MANAGING

YOUR INHERITANCE

STEPHEN GADSDEN
PHILIP GATES

 McGraw-Hill
Ryerson

Toronto New York Burr Ridge Bangkok Bogotá Caracas
Lisbon London Madrid Mexico City Milan New Delhi
Seoul Singapore Sydney Taipei

McGraw-Hill
Ryerson Limited

A Subsidiary of The *McGraw-Hill* Companies

300 Water Street, Whitby, Ontario L1N 9B6
http://www.mcgrawhill.ca

ISBN: 0-07-552772-3
1234567890 BBM 901987654321098
Printed and bound in Canada

Care has been taken to trace ownership of copyright material contained in this text; however, the publisher will welcome any information that enables them to rectify any reference or credit for subsequent editions.

This book has been written for a lay audience. The technical legal definitions of certain terms, such as "heirs" (intestate distributees determinable solely upon the death of the decedent) and "beneficiaries," have been set aside in favour of the more common, connotative meanings of the words.

This publication is designed to provide accurate and authoritative information in regard to the subject matter covered. It is published with the understanding that the publisher and authors are not engaged in rendering legal, accounting, or other professional service. If legal advice or other professional advice, including financial, is required, the services of a competent professional person should be sought. The tax system is constantly changing. Consequently, the tax discussions in this book have been designed for general applicability.

Canadian Cataloguing in Publication Data
Gadsden, Stephen The new heir's guide to managing your inheritance
Includes index.
ISBN 0-07-552772-3
1. Finance, Personal - Canada. 2. Inheritance and succession - Canada. 3. Saving and investment - Canada. I. Gates, Philip A. II. Title.
HG179.G327 1997   332.024'01   C97-931723-1

Publisher: Joan Homewood
Editor: Erin Moore
Production Coordinator: Jennifer Burnell
Editorial Services: Drew McCarthy
Cover Design: Sharon Matthews
Interior Design/Composition: Pages Design
Printer: Best Book Manufacturers

CONTENTS

INTRODUCTION

❧

THE BASICS OF INHERITED WEALTH

YOU MIGHT NOT SEE YOURSELF as an heir, but think again. Nearly 8 million Canadians will leave bequests averaging $80,000 over the next 20 years, ranging in size from modest to multimillion-dollar estates. Consider the following:

1. Do your parents own a home?
2. Is their home paid for?
3. Do your parents own stocks?
4. Does each of your parents have a valid will?
5. Are there any other likely heirs?

If you answered yes to any of these questions, you may be among the "new heirs" — baby boomer children of the first large-scale middle class in history — who stand to inherit about 1 trillion dollars from their savings-oriented, depression-era parents. These savings, combined with the twin effects of relatively low taxes on capital gains and economic boom times, form the unprecedented projected transfer of wealth.

Inheriting money doesn't sound like a problem, so you're probably thinking: Why do I need a book to find out how to spend my inheritance? But *spending* your inheritance is exactly what you shouldn't do.

Here's the problem: Unlike their frugal parents, boomers have exhibited the lowest savings rate in recent history, only about 4% of income. In addition, this generation — you know who you are — has amassed the highest debt in history, not counting mortgage and credit card debt.

Your twin temptations: pay off debt and then create new debt. Old habits die hard, so our challenge is to help you understand how to conserve and increase your new assets.

But even before you inherit, or while you are in the process of going through probate (the formal transfer of your inheritance), you'll face many new issues, from dealing with executors to conquering the complexities of estate planning.

We designed this book to carry you through the process.

THE NEW HEIR's PRIMER

The management of inherited wealth can be organized using three basic concepts:
- Inheriting the past,
- Maximizing the present, and
- Providing for the future.

New heirs inherit more than money. There are tremendous psychological implications of inherited wealth. As an heir, you must deal with feelings of guilt and responsibility, as well as family "silver strings" which tie the inheritor to the grantor. You must also control the temptation to immediately change your current lifestyle because of the inheritance. New heirs are also confronted with a variety of complex legal and tax issues at an emotionally distraught time.

Once the estate is settled, you should develop an asset management plan which will maximize the current and future value of your inheritance. Managing a lump-sum transfer raises asset allocation and capital preservation concerns that differ in focus from typical personal finance issues.

Finally, your inheritance presents you with both opportunity and responsibility. The receipt of an inheritance marks a change in your life, in terms of your family, your finances, or both. As a result, you now need to consider your own estate plan and the way you want to use your capital to provide for the future of your family and our society.

In the three main parts of the book, we will explore each of these concepts.

Although most of us think of heirs and heiresses as the super-rich who already have substantial amounts of money to throw around, during the coming decades we will see a new type of inheritor. Many will be middle-aged or even nearing retirement. Some will be younger baby boomers with a propensity to spend. Other inheritors will be restricted by trusts, such as those set up for college education or those established for control of family members' access to assets.

Together you are the "new heirs." You face the prospect of managing lump sums of inherited money although you may never have learned good money management habits for yourself. Your challenge: To preserve the inheritance and increase its value rather than squander it.

HOW MUCH IS MUCH?

All inheritances are not created equal. Although current predictions show the average inheritance at $80,000, the amount any new heir actually receives can vary dramatically. As a result, the right advice to follow depends on whether your inheritance is modest or in the millions. To apply the general rules to your specific situation, "4M Formula" checklists appear throughout the book. The 4M Formula summarizes advice according to the size of your inheritance. Our cutoff points follow — but, of course, what you consider "modest" or "major" depends on you.

- Modest *(less than $50,000)*
- Moderate *($50,000–$250,000)*
- Major *($250,000–$1,000,000)*
- Millions *(over $1,000,000)*

If you have been living a high lifestyle, even an inheritance of $200,000 may seem fairly modest; conversely, if your inheritance is significantly more than your family's annual income, its effects could be major, regardless of its size.

THE 4M FORMULA

Here's a brief example of differences based on the size of the inheritance, or what we call our 4M Formulas:

Modest: *(Less than $50,000)*
Probate: May not be required.
Lifestyle: Minimum changes.
Estate Plan: Living trust and living will.
Action: Secure your retirement and your children's and grandchildren's education.
Investments: RRSP, principal residence, and RESP.

Moderate *($50,000–$250,000)*
Probate: Probate or living trust.
Lifestyle: Ease some of your cash flow concerns, but do not retire. Consider your tax position and your estate plan.
Estate Plan: Living trust and living will. Consider spousal rollovers, utilization of Capital Gains Deduction and family trusts.
Action: Develop a conservative asset allocation plan.
Investments: RRSP, principal residence, mutual fund, and RESP.

Major: *($250,000–$1,000,000)*
Probate: You are probably the beneficiary of a complex estate plan, and now you clearly see the need to create one of your own.

Lifestyle: Even if you may not retire, these resources may allow you to change careers or engage in other pursuits you've dreamed about.

Estate Plan: Consider family trusts, estate freezing, utilization of the Capital Gains Deduction, and spousal rollovers.

Action: Plan for taxes, allocate your assets, and maximize your inheritance. SEEK PROFESSIONAL ADVICE.

Investments: Real estate, stocks, bonds, RRSP, RESP, metals, and mutual funds.

Millions *(Over $1,000,000)*

Probate: You have probably been part of the estate planning process as a trust beneficiary or the recipient of asset transfers for most of your life.

Lifestyle: Many options available to choose from.

Estate Plan: Set up irrevocable trusts for each of your children and grandchildren. Consider spousal rollovers, estate freezing and utilization of the Capital Gains Deduction.

Action: Establish your plan objectives and priorities and then work closely with a team of advisors to develop your estate plan, allocate your assets, and minimize your tax liability. You can flow your capital to venture capital and charitable organizations. Be alert because the positive opportunities provided by wealth can have equally powerful costs and trade-offs.

Investments: Real estate, growth stocks, bonds, international funds, metals, minerals, venture capital, RRSP and RESP, and always the family business and family farm, and equalizing the tax burden over as many taxpayers as possible.

THE FIRST YEAR

The challenges and dangers facing new heirs are especially strong immediately after inheriting. By avoiding temptation and planning ahead, you can successfully navigate the transition.

Be aware of emotional pitfalls. Acknowledge and deal with the emotional aspects of inherited wealth, especially the wealth of your parents. Examine how susceptible you may be at an emotionally charged time to solicitations for your money that don't best suit your needs. Seek out dispassionate independent advice.

Look out for silver strings which bind inheritors to their wealth. Dealing with the psychological aspects is critical to successfully managing the wealth. The emotional family ties that inherited wealth represents can take their toll. If parents were overbearing, middle-aged "children" may rebel by spending their parents' money. A wise inheritor learns to focus on his or her own needs rather than allow the family strings to tug. Dance to your own drummer.

Be prepared when you receive your inheritance. If you believe your parents, spouse, or relatives will leave you money, it's prudent, not ghoulish, to know the basics beforehand.

THE NEW HEIR'S CHECKLIST

Here is a short list of suggestions for beginning to manage your inheritance successfully, especially during your first year as a new heir.
- Be aware of emotional pitfalls.
- Be aware of psychological silver strings.
- Plan ahead for inheritance.
- Seek out competent professional advisors.
- Discuss inheritance matters with spouse and other significant family.
- Learn to deal with trusts.
- Focus on preserving your capital.
- Work to minimize taxes with professional advice.
- Be a conservative investor and seek out professional advice.
- Protect your capital from inflation.
- Start good habits now.

By familiarizing yourself with the estate settlement process now, you will be better able to discuss estate plans with your family. You can even fantasize about what you might do with a given amount of money; for example — so much to pay off debts, so much to children's education, so much to investments, and so much to charity. Then, commit your thoughts to paper and tuck them away so that you'll have a plan prepared at a contemplative, rather than emotional time.

Dealing with trusts can present special challenges. If your money is held in trust, you'll want to stay active in the management of the trusts, even if only on an informal basis with the trustees. Try to get the income disbursed in full every year. Do not leave it to accumulate, because undistributed income becomes *corpus*, or principal, and will not be available for your use unless the trust specifically allows for its distribution to you.

Work to minimize taxes, both for the estate, if you can, and on your income from the estate. If your family politics allow, try to help your parents structure their estate to the best advantage to minimize taxes on their respective estates. For larger estates try working with your parents on their estate plans (if they're willing), to develop family trusts, estate freezing and use of their maximum Capital Gains Deductions.

Focus on preserving your capital, especially for the first year or two after you inherit. Even if you spend the income from the assets, preserve the capital base for growth in the future. If you spend the inheritance now, without planning, you will live to regret it later.

Be a conservative investor. You should pause before undertaking any investment or other activity that would put your capital at risk. For example, if you have $300,000 and you put it in a safe but long-term investment it might earn $30,000 a year. Depending on where you live and whether you own a home, you could almost retire on that amount. You could also easily run through $300,000 in a year-long spending spree and be left with nothing.

Protect your capital from inflation with solid growth-oriented investments, rather than looking to "make a killing" in high-risk, high-growth investments. The myriad of deals that entrepreneurs offer provide enticements for the newly moneyed. We would all like to make a killing in the stock market, but the reality is, for all but the most sophisticated and active investor, the most prudent path is to diversify with conservative, growth-oriented opportunities.

FINANCIAL DECISION-MAKING

To ease financial decision-making, be mindful of the following investment issues:

• *Cash Flow:* The timing of cash inflows, whether your income is from your investments or disbursements.

• *Taxes:* The potential tax consequences, which can improve or hamper the expected return from your income or an investment.

• *Growth:* The expected returns on an investment and the opportunity for an investment to expand the capital base, such as the increase in the value of an asset over time.

• *Risk:* Simply put, the potential for loss related to an investment. Risk is typically inversely related to growth or expected return. Risk can be further divided into two types: systematic risk related to the holding of a specific asset, such as Bell Canada stock; and non systematic risk, relating to overall market performance, such as the entire stock market.

• *Liquidity:* The ease of converting an investment to cash, such as the difference between the time it takes to withdraw money from your large savings account and receiving the proceeds from selling your home.

- *Diversification:* The mix of assets that comprise the investor's total wealth. An asset base consisting only of local real estate investments is poorly diversified because the entire base is subject to loss from a downturn in that real estate market.
- *Personal Preference:* To prevent investors from regretting even rational business decisions, it is imperative that inheritors take their personal desires and preferences into account, such as the desire to retain a particular asset because of its high sentimental value despite a low market value.

New heirs face the additional challenge of considering these investment parameters when combining their existing assets — however scant — with their inheritances.

AN EXAMPLE

Take the example of Wendy,[1] who inherited a house and Alcan stock from her mother's estate. With her $55,000 annual income, she is already self-sufficient; therefore, she does not need more liquidity or immediate cash flow. Because she already owns real estate, the addition of inherited property would mean that real property would comprise, for example, 75% of her asset mix. To be diversified, she would want to sell the house, unless she has an overriding personal preference to keep the property. With the funds from the sale of the house, she could invest in a variety of bonds; a quality large-cap mutual fund; an international equity fund; and a money market account. These changes improve her portfolio's diversification and limit risk yet provide for growth.

A NEW HEIR'S CHALLENGES

1.   Avoid the temptation to change your lifestyle immediately, and recognize that there are both obvious and subtle psychological implications of inheriting wealth.

2.   Discuss estate planning with your family. Remember that you are not the only one to face problems with parents or siblings and to learn from the experiences of others.

3.   Gain an understanding of the estate process before you are forced to deal with executors and trustees at emotional times.

4.   Learn the fundamentals of cash flow, budgeting, retirement planning, and taxes to stay in control of your new and old assets.

5.   If you are the beneficiary of a trust, learn to deal with the special challenges of trusts.

---

[1] All characters in this book, with the exception of public figures, are fictitious.

6. Plan your estate. Even if you already have a will, the addition of your inheritance is cause enough for you and your spouse to reexamine your estate and consider the multitude of options available to you.

7. Develop a professional team to advise you on your legal, financial, and other affairs.

8. Consider the trade-offs of risk, growth, liquidity, and diversification in allocating your assets.

9. Learn from the successes and failures of other new heirs trying to manage their inheritances.

10. Take control of your wealth and direct the flow of capital to responsible uses, if you so want.

EMOTIONAL WEALTH

When we meet our inherited fortunes, often in those vulnerable months following the death of a parent, we are usually least equipped to deal with them. Whether one has lived a lifetime with the expectation of inheriting resources or the possibility is a new one, preparation can save emotional, as well as financial, expense.

To anticipate your inheritance intelligently, incorporate good budgeting, savings, spending, and investment habits now. These habits, along with your plan, will pave the way for managing your inheritance positively.

In addition, you may want to consider the responsibilities as well as the privileges of wealth. According to the old school, *noblesse oblige*, or the obligations of wealth, included using the money to create good, generally through philanthropy. But another school has a better idea, to direct the economy toward positive change through the *socially responsible use of capital*.

While an inheritance offers you personal and family benefits, your new money also affords you the opportunity to make a difference to the community. Just look at how the environmental movement has reached down to the checkout line, where many times when you buy groceries, you're queried, "Paper or plastic?" Consider what would happen if every new heir put 10% of her or his inheritance into investments that underwrote positive social goals — that would mean $30 billion forging a new path.

These possibilities have barely been contemplated by policy makers. From views on the meaning of wealth to the effects on their own children, the $3 trillion transfer of wealth can make agents of change of a vast new group of inheritors. The baby boom generation has changed everything it's touched. With capital in hand, this generation could well reset personal, social, and political priorities for decades to come. As a new heir, you can lead them.

PART ONE

❧

INHERITING THE PAST

Of comfort no man speak:
Let's talk of graves, of worms, and epitaphs;
Make dust our paper, and with rainy eyes
Write sorrow on the bosom of the earth.
Let's choose executors, and talk of wills.
                    — *Shakespeare,* King Richard II

1

♣

AVOIDING
INHERITANCE PITFALLS

SO YOU JUST GOT an inheritance. Time to get rid of that old car sitting in the driveway, or maybe time to get a new driveway. Tired of eating at those same restaurants and wearing those same old outfits? Already planning a trip to Europe? Not so fast! The temptations that come with the windfall of an inheritance are like those facing a lottery winner. Like the lottery winner, to make the most of what you get, avoiding the temptation to make overnight changes is key.

Unless your money is in trust, you'll receive your inheritance in a lump sum. So before you go out and buy a new wardrobe, let's take a quick look at the difference, even without inflationary effects, between buying a $100,000 Mercedes Benz and putting the same money in an equity mutual fund earning an average of 7% over the next ten years:

	500SL	Mutual Fund
Day 1	$100,000	$100,000
Day 2	90,000	100,019
Year 2	75,000	114,981
Year 5	55,000	141,763
Year 10	30,000	200,966

If you can't resist the temptation to spend some of the money immediately, then at least do it systematically. A few suggestions:

1. *Take 5% of your inheritance and go crazy.* Buy something you always wanted, take a trip, get some new clothes, pick out some nice presents for your family, throw a party — you get the idea. The point is, get it out of your system, but keep it under control. (With a large inheritance, don't spend the entire 5% at once. Put it in a special savings account and consider it your discretionary money, to use with or without discretion.)

2. *Pay off your expensive debts.* Credit card debts and other debts with double-digit interest rates cost more than an investment will normally earn you. It is safe to assume that you'll save money if you retire such expensive debts. Paying off these debts serves two purposes: You're relieved of the psychological burden of having the debt, and you've made a financially rational decision since the debt costs more than you can safely earn with the same money.

Two cautions apply. First, if you've been a habitual overuser of credit, simply paying the bills won't solve the problem. You'll have to retire most of your cards and stringently examine the causes and solutions to overspending.

Second, if you have a mortgage or other less long-term, lower interest obligations, don't pay them immediately. Examine whether you can achieve higher returns from investments than the cost of interest on the debt. Don't forget to take taxes into account — as you'll owe different amounts of tax on dividends, interest and capital gains. And, if you retire your mortgage, you'll lose your income tax deduction for the interest portion of the payment linked to a business or property investment.

Although you may later decide to exchange less costly debt for freedom, don't do so immediately. Having the bank as your co-investor in property in the form of a mortgage, for example, can save your finances in a market downturn or natural disaster. The upside of retiring mortgage debt is that the interest paid over the life of a loan can double the cost of the house.

3. *Consider starting or increasing savings for your retirement.* Building your Registered Retirement Savings Plan (RRSP) provides multiple benefits. First, a contribution to an RRSP is a conscious commitment to save for the future. Second, you can defer income taxes on the funds placed in an RRSP. Third, if you've put off retirement planning, or, if you've underfunded your RRSP, you can now pay up to the maximum allowed by law. Fourth, because a cash withdrawal from an RRSP triggers tax exposure, you'll have a built-in incentive not to withdraw funds, as compared to a savings or money market account. Fifth, these funds will increase pre-tax dollars; therefore, retirement savings earn compound interest for you on money that would otherwise go to taxes. Even if all of your other investments turn sour, with a solid RRSP, you won't starve in your old age, as long as you leave the retirement funds intact.

4. *Set up a Registered Education Savings Plan (RESP) for your children or grandchildren.* If you have children and have not started saving for their education, now's the time to put aside money specifically for this purpose. If your inheritance provides enough money to educate your children, but college is a few years off, you can set up an RESP for each child, funded each year with your $5,000 contribution. Actual funds in the RESP compound tax-free and will be taxable only to the beneficiary on withdrawal.

Each of these suggestions is a safe way to let off some spending steam without causing you to mismanage in haste your inheritance, to your later regret. The technicalities of money management, taxes, asset allocation, trusts, and estate planning are explained in Parts Two and Three of the book, where these and other choices for the management of your wealth are discussed in detail. First, it's important that you get into the proper mindset by dealing with the psychological aspects of inheriting wealth.

THE ROLE OF THE INHERITANCE IN YOUR LIFE

Just because you have new assets does not necessarily mean that you have a new life. When the inheritance arrives, or even before it gets to you, you need to consider the effect the inheritance *could* have on your life. Is it enough to have a good time tomorrow? Is it enough for your future retirement? Is it enough to retire now? Does it carry obligations and responsibilities?

THE 4M FORMULA FOR LIFESTYLE

Modest:

Follow the advice in this chapter closely. The majority of your inheritance should be going toward your children's education and/or your retirement plan.

Moderate:

Depending on the size of your inheritance, you may be able to supplement your current income nicely, prepare your family's future, and enjoy less of a cash flow crunch. Consider the advice in this chapter.

Major:

You have many options and opportunities. You can supplement your income and improve your standard of living, or you can take the opportunity to make a make a transition to a new career or a new location. Consider the advice in this chapter, then focus on your asset allocation discussed in Part Two of this book.

Millions:

Don't run out and quit your job yet. You have been given the opportunity to revisit dreams which may now be attainable; but remember, the income of one million dollars, after taxes and inflationary effects, might not support the living standard of a high-paying career. Seriously consider your alternatives, expected cash flows, and your asset allocation. Age plays a role as well, since having money is no substitute for the psychological rewards of career competence. Do enjoy some of your discretionary money while you're planning.

To identify the potential role of the inheritance in your life, begin a written journal, allowing yourself to list your dreams, however far-fetched. Order your dreams and aspirations in terms of your personal sense of priorities. Pick the top three or four and see whether the money you have inherited will assist you to realize these goals.

Not all dreams can be attained through wealth, but you may be able to revitalize some long-forgotten desires. One fifty-year-old heir who inherited a fortune said, "I'd given up my teenage dream to be an astronaut, but one day I realized that in a few years I could probably *buy* a trip into space."

Allow your imagination free reign before you check it against practical reality. Then ask if you have provided for your children, your future? Do you have political, charitable, or other socially responsible activities to support? Dream your dreams, but do a reality check before you start spending.

WHY BOTHER MANAGING?

What is the point of all this talk about responsibly managing your inheritance anyway? It is *your* inheritance, so what's the big deal if you spend the whole thing tomorrow for a good time? Good reasons exist to manage the inheritance for yourself, and if not for yourself, for future generations.

Yourself

If you spend an entire inheritance to have a good time, a modest amount won't last long, and then you'll be back where you started with only yourself to blame.

However, the inheritance will continue to grow if you use your current income to maintain your current lifestyle. If you are now forty and achieve 8% returns compounded annually on $50,000 until you're sixty-five, you will have $367,009 to live out the rest of a potentially nonworking life, not to mention any other savings, retirement benefits or pension income that you might receive. Even if you assume 4% inflation, the present value of the amount is $135,688. That thought alone should provide you with longer-term relief and happiness than any short-lived spending spree.

If you inherit a large amount of money, you also inherit opportunity, the opportunity to control the flow of capital. By responsibly managing this control, you can improve your life, the lives of your family, and the world around you. Not only do you have the opportunity to save for your future, but you can supplement your current income to support activities and causes of interest to you. You also can learn to face the challenges of inherited wealth before they darken an otherwise bright outlook on life.

Society

If the personal argument isn't convincing enough, let's try the socially responsible approach. Imagine if every new heir mismanaged or squandered his or her inheritance. The cumulative effect of such irresponsibility on a nation already burdened with a $600 billion debt could be devastating. In effect, past savings would be spent currently at the cost of the future.

Of course, you might argue that it is virtually impossible that all $1 trillion of the inheritance boom would be simultaneously mismanaged. If you do it, why shouldn't the next guy, and his sister, and her friend. Just remember that every well-planned investment decision that you make not only provides for yourself but is an investment in the future of our economy.

PUTTING THE INHERITANCE IN PERSPECTIVE

A common pitfall for new inheritors, especially those who have grown accustomed to living from paycheque to paycheque, is to exaggerate the extent of their inherited wealth. They may use it to live on rather than to supplement earnings or may mistakenly treat the lump-sum receipt as an adjustment to their permanent income stream and spend accordingly. You should establish a preliminary budget and gain a clear picture of the changes in your tax position in light of your inheritance before you make any rash decisions. With a "quick and dirty" budget, you can immediately see whether the inheritance will simply supplement your lifestyle or replace it.

For most working heirs, given the projected average "baby boom" inheritance of $80,000, the primary use should be for retirement funds. In particular, if a salaried person has enjoyed a "live today, pay tomorrow," high-cash-flow life, the inheritance could spell the difference between a difficult retirement and a secure one.

Far too many new heirs have blown their entire fortunes. One new heir spent her whole inheritance on a winter trip to Hawaii that she "desperately needed for her life." Within two weeks of returning, her prior stress level had returned, her income had not improved, and her retirement fund remained virtually empty. Had she invested the funds, she could have taken a more modest summer vacation and increased the assets to maintain her current lifestyle after she retired. Instead, she acted as if the inheritance represented a permanent change in her income that she would enjoy every year and let it vanish forever in short-term gratification.

For some fortunate heirs at the upper end of the inheritance scale, the inheritance serves as a new source of income which replaces the need to work. As is the case with many wealthy inheritors, the heir may already have been enjoying a steady income from trusts or family gifts. With the added funds, the new heir now has the opportunity to focus on favourite causes; set up a charitable donations budget; or enter the world of political donations, with the associated heady access to the powerful and famous. These heirs should take time to understand the special issues related to dealing with trusts; creating sophisticated estate plans; and making responsible venture capital investments.

For other heirs, whose position falls somewhere in the middle, the inheritance is large enough to use some of the income or principal now, but too small to replace a salary. The extra flexibility provided by the supplemental income may be enough to allow the heir to choose a new job or a new career. Or these heirs could consider reducing their work time to enjoy more free time. One study has found that 23% of people inheriting more than $250,000 stop working, as compared to less than 5% of those receiving modest inheritances.

WEALTH

If it has not affected you already, inheriting money, especially if it is a lot of money, will change your life in both obvious and subtle ways. An awareness of these potential effects, whether or not they actually do apply to you, will help you to confront or avoid them. Although in our culture it's commonplace to assume "the more money the better," a writer once observed, "To suppose, as we all suppose, that we could be rich and not behave the way the rich behave, is like saying that we could drink all day and stay sober."

Wealth has been the obsession of writers, musicians, psychologists, and sociologists for decades. The futility of wealth is a recurrent theme among recent thinkers, yet many people still dream obsessively about money.

Often inherited wealth, granted without discipline, unearned except by birthright, leaves a person crippled emotionally or intellectually. Michael Crichton may have put it best in the American film, *Jurassic Park*, in a monologue of the questioning scientist Ian Malcolm:

> I will tell you what I am talking about," he said. "Most kinds of power require a substantial sacrifice by whoever wants the power. There is an apprenticeship, a discipline lasting many years. Whatever kind of power you want: President of the company; Black belt in karate; Spiritual guru. Whatever it is you seek, you have to put in the time, the practice, the effort. You must give up a lot to get it. It has to be very important to you. And once you have attained it, it is your power. It can't be given away: it resides in you. It is literally the result of your discipline.
>
> Now, what is interesting about this process is that, by the time someone has acquired the ability to kill with his bare hands, he has also matured to the point where he won't use it unwisely. So that kind of power has built-in control. The discipline of getting the power changes you so that you won't abuse it.
>
> But scientific power is like inherited wealth: attained without discipline.

This lack of discipline has differentiated many dilettante heirs from successful investors and entrepreneurs. Heirs all too often develop a distorted sense of themselves and others, not having experienced the effort, cultivated the relationships, or attained the leadership associated with achieving the wealth firsthand.

Distorted perception is not the only shortcoming of wealth. Others have warned of the inability of money to satisfy the most basic of human desires — love. The Beatles express the sentiment in "Can't Buy Me Love" and Bruce Springsteen sings about it in "Ain't Got You." Money, they warn, is not the answer to a satisfying life.

But it could obviously provide you with some of the comforts on the way. There's an old saying, "Behind a rich man there stands a devil, behind a poor man there stands two." It would be foolish to suggest that in today's society there are no benefits to having money. Money can bring comfort, opportunity, and power. For the right price, fine dining, fast cars, and exquisite service await. Even legal, health and retirement concerns are affected by wealth. In fact, control of the flow of capital provides the ability to affect industry, create opportunity for others, and better the community. Or, it simply allows you to achieve your personal goals.

Beware, the stream of power between you and the control of money flows both ways. Should the day come when the money controls you, all the benefits of wealth are soon washed away.

Some heirs resent their wealth. Having already won the game society scores with wealth, they feel they have nothing left to compete or strive for. In *The Fountainhead*, Ayn Rand describes this phenomenon best through the monologue of a fictional wealthy American heir, Mitch Layton, who attacks the publisher of a newspaper empire on whose board Mitch sits:

> ... I come to a meeting of stockholders and he treats us like flunkies. Isn't my money as good as his? Don't I own a hunk of his damn paper? I could teach him a thing or two about journalism. I have ideas. What's he so damn arrogant about? Just because he made that fortune himself? Does he have to be such a damn snob just because he came from Hell's Kitchen? It isn't other people's fault if they weren't lucky enough to be born in Hell's Kitchen to rise out of! Nobody understands what a terrible handicap it is to be born rich. Because people just take for granted that because you were born that way you'd just be no good if you weren't. What I mean is if I'd had [his] breaks, I'd be twice as rich as he is by now and three times as famous. But he's so conceited he doesn't realize this at all!

This warped perspective can arise from insecurity common among young heirs. They judge themselves, as others do, by wealth, and yet they never truly feel it is their own. Karl Marx argued that because they did not share in the creation of the wealth, a sense of alienation accompanies the wealth. With wealth as the prime measure of accomplishment, they can find no basis for an unbiased evaluation of their own self-worth.

Whether it tends to bring happiness or despair, money, a mere material object, has its limits. As Henry David Thoreau observed, "Superfluous wealth can buy superfluities only. Money is not required to buy one necessity of the soul." Your wealth may give you the time to paint, but it may not make you a great painter.

PSYCHOLOGICAL PITFALLS

Heirs have historically been thought to deal with their wealth as do princes, in luxurious enjoyment. But recent research has focused on the negative psychological effects associated with inheriting substantial sums of money. Although responses vary with each case, you are better prepared for your own inheritance if you are aware of the psychological responses common to many of the heirs.

Regret

A common response among first-generation heirs of entrepreneurial wealth is regret — regret that the parent creating the business focused so much on monetary issues and not enough on life. These heirs often wish that they had been given at least a portion of the value of their inheritance in the form of attention and wisdom. This response is particularly acute where families have defined themselves by their wealth.

Immaturity

In families with more than one child, inheriting wealth almost inevitably involves settling outstanding emotional and family positional issues along with settling the wealth. Unfortunately, many families with high net worth suffer from various disfunctionalities that compound this emotionally fraught period. The problem is that in such wealthy families, the money is frequently substituted for expressions of love or achievement as the token of exchange.

For some, the expectation and fact of substantial inheritance results in delayed (sometimes permanent) emotional development. Many inheritors are spared much of life's challenge, their money providing a cocoon that sometimes frees them from everyday problems but inhibits their full growth as personalities. Second generation inheritors may also have difficulty with self-discipline. Many heirs find great difficulty in focusing because they have so many options and because they can change directions at will. Self-discipline is necessary not only for work, but also for building significant relationships. Because of this, some heirs seem to act as though they are four even when they are forty-year-old private investors.

Boredom

Inheritors also often experience boredom. They miss seeing real-life challenges because wealth brings so many available options. In fact, the same challenges facing others also face the heirs. The difference is that the heirs may have more immediate resources available to meet those challenges or seek new ones.

The other reaction to the flood of decisions suddenly available to new heirs is paralysis, the inability to make life choices because of the multitude of options. Heirs find themselves unable to plan a career or even a weekend because decisions seem impossible in the face of so many options.

In reality, plans must be made the same way they were made before the inheritance, hopefully with added creativity. Now more of the plans you make may be realistic, but time, if not money, limits us all, even the wealthy.

Authoritarianism

Some heirs unknowingly develop a demented view of their own power and an exaggerated self-esteem, basing their relationships with other people on the experience they might have had with servants or the deference afforded to their families when they were younger because they were rich. These habits, in turn, result in the heir having problems with the use of power. With the positional power afforded in our society to those with wealth, heirs too often become petty tyrants without realizing it. Like celebrities, rich people rarely hear the truth from others.

As expressed by Michael Crichton, when heirs receive wealth without the discipline ordinarily required to create it, situations arise where personalities have power, in the form of wealth, but lack the personal power and control to exercise it wisely.

It is important to recognize that money alone will not gain you true respect. If you do acquire power through your inherited wealth, remember that although money may afford control over others, people, in the end, respond to people.

Paranoia

Inheritors often feel guilty about their wealth, while they also become suspicious because they are so often the targets of others' material desires. Relationships become difficult to establish because of feelings of mistrust. In addition, women inheritors may face additional problems, from the difficulty of finding a suitable mate to the fact that they are left out of family business and investment decision making. These feelings often accompany and exaggerate the other negative emotions facing the heirs.

This fear may be overcome by maintaining control over your wealth. If you do not flaunt your wealth or make it a defining characteristic of yourself, then people will more likely respond to you rather than your money. In this sense, paranoia about your highly visible wealth may be a self-fulfilling prophecy.

Inadequacy

Autonomy and identity are often hard to establish and maintain when a family has so defined itself by its wealth, rather than accomplishments. Studies show that among the wealthy, self-esteem is often inadequate. Inheritors often fear failure, especially in the area of vocation, since they've never been forced to earn their own living and don't really know whether they could.

Where so much emphasis is put on money, it becomes the only value of worth. And there is always someone more worthy because there is always someone more wealthy.

While these experiences are drawn primarily from the very wealthy, even more modest inheritors will experience some of these feelings, especially in a society where poverty and hopelessness are visibly present.

AWARENESS ENABLES AVOIDANCE

While hopefully not all new heirs will be overcome by temptation or experience all of the above problems (especially since the amounts most inherit will be modest), the problems that wealthy inheritors experience could colour your relationship to your inheritance and to others.

The happiness and despair borne by wealth have been well documented. The polarity of possible outcomes makes clear that the money itself is not the determining factor. Rather, your attitude and self-confidence define the effects of your new-found riches on your life.

2

𝔸

FAMILY MATTERS

The Inheritors, The Film,
Act I, Scene i
INT. — KITCHEN — 1958 — CHRISTMAS
[Fade in:]
[JOAN runs to kiss FATHER hello while STEVE tries to cover up his report card.]
FATHER
Hi, honey pie, straight A's again?
He reaches into his pocket with one hand.
FATHER
[Cont.]
Steve?
Steve reluctantly hands over his report card, hangs in the doorway. Father hands Joan two dollars as he studies Steve's grades. He tucks his wallet back into his pocket.
FATHER
[Cont.]
Well, at least you got one B — in P.E.
[CUT TO:]   INT. — PARENTS' HOUSE — PRESENT
Dressed in black, Steve and Joan sit at the kitchen table, holding copies of their dad's will.
STEVE
Why am I surprised he left you the house and stocks and me the Mercedes and his library? He was always shelling out dollars to you.
JOAN
I earned that money. Besides, I can't help it if I was a better student.
STEVE
It doesn't take a genius to see he always favoured you — about four times as much. [He holds up the will.]
JOAN
Steve, he knows you love collecting — you can't place a value on that. [Steve throws the will on the table, rises.]

STEVE
Excuse me. I've got to get started boxing up my inheritance — two hundred old *National Geographics.*
[FADE OUT]

The nonfiction reality is that death often catches us by surprise. The grieving heirs are often called upon to confront one another around property issues, discussions of which all too often substitute for much-needed, healthy grieving, and as a result, conflict ensues.

Whatever the previous family dynamic, roles are written large at death. In families that dealt poorly with conflict when the parent was alive, property struggles often break out. One family fought over a used toaster at a will reading. In another, a father had his contentious children flip coins for every object of personal property, from used clothes to antique furniture, that any of them wanted.

No matter the financial position of the family — from working class to wealthy — the control of money represents power and control within the family. In that respect, the family mirrors society. In some families, this power and control may be shared in a model of functional family management. In others, money is mistakenly substituted for love, leading to disfunction and miscommunication.

The level of family trust will also govern the extent to which the family is able to cope with preparing in advance for the death of a parent. Parents who maturely face the fact that life on earth is limited and set about to square up their financial affairs leave their children in a better financial position than parents who deny their own mortality and delay settling their affairs.

The ideal model involves parents who are willing to discuss estate plans openly, especially with children. Two-thirds of parents surveyed said that they already discussed their wills with their children or meant to. If children are allowed to give their points of view directly to their parents while parents are still alive, parents are empowering children to carry on as the next generation in the family. According to one survey of potential heirs, 58% thought prior knowledge of an inheritance's details would avoid conflict and controversy later.

But inheritance often replicates lifetime family patterns of dealing with money. Financial secrets represent financial control. In families where children have learned only the minimum about family finances, aging parents aren't likely to suddenly become spouting sources of information as they approach death.

In fact, one reason so many people die *intestate*, without any will or estate plan, is their inability or unwillingness to face up to their own mortality. In addition, as long as a parent can dangle the possibility of "prospects," the parent can keep the child's attention. As middle-aged people struggle with their own often precarious existences and face coping with the demands of aging parents, sometimes, it's sad to say, parents feel that only the prospect of getting their money keeps the kids coming home.

By contrast, there is an implicit, though not-often articulated, promise between generations that if the younger generation cares for the older one, then the younger generation can expect to inherit. Unfortunately, as marriage and family life has eroded, introducing second and even third spouses, new parameters must be considered. Studies show that most people plan to leave the bulk of their estate to their spouses; if a parent has remarried, children often fear being left out in the cold.

Families can approach intergenerational issues proactively, sitting down and sharing the details so that there are no surprises after the funeral.

Or, they can follow the film script model, where in addition to death, property arrangements are a grab-bag of surprises, often unpleasant.

PROACTIVE FAMILY ESTATE PLANNING

PARENTAL WILLINGNESS TO DISCUSS THEIR PLANS

A fundamental issue that must be addressed is how to get a family to talk about death and property. While some families do it by the book, sitting down and tackling the tough issues involved in discussing mortality and the succession of generations, don't be surprised if your request to talk about your parents' estate plans (or even their estate) is met with stony silence or even anger.

While everyone knows that they will eventually die, most want to put off thinking about the specifics of time. How often have you heard the phrase, "If I should die..." — as if there were an alternative!

Preparing an estate plan confronts even the most practical and worldly adults with teary-eyed issues. Parents have been known to shudder at the thought of their otherwise capable and respected children taking over the family business.

So, while the ideal scenario involves a rational discussion of key issues — the location of the will, the choice of executor, the designation of beneficiaries, and the preparation of a tax plan — the reality is often different. You may have to be satisfied with knowing little or nothing of your parents' plans. Or, at best, bits and pieces may emerge over the years as you visit other family graves or discuss the deaths of family members.

By contrast, older people increasingly share their thoughts about taking extraordinary life-saving measures in the event of lingering illness. Because of modern medical technology and the spectre of lingering indefinitely, the preparation of living wills or other instructions regarding medical decisions about life support and the management of one's financial affairs has become commonplace. Individuals now regularly commit their wishes to legally binding instructions in the form of both durable powers of attorney and living wills.

Even though your parents may resist discussing the money and executor portions of their estate wishes, you may find them more receptive if you express your concern about their well-being in the end. But don't press these delicate issues or use health issues as a wedge to open the estate discussion. Often, as people approach death or sense that their time is passing, they will undertake preparing their estate plans, a most private and personal activity. They may not necessarily want to discuss these plans with their children.

One estate recipient shared her experience:

> My own mother loved life too much to relish planning for her end. But after losing two brothers, she was motivated to put her affairs in order. When Mama died, she managed to go in style. She hadn't done everything by the book, but she had taken sufficient steps so that her children could manage closing her affairs.
>
> Mother took great care to prepare a properly drawn holographic will, complete with the disposition of most of her property. In retrospect, I realized that she had been preparing her estate plan for about two years, as her many questions about family heirlooms suggested. She had subtly established who wanted what, then made sure her plans fairly distributed the various items. Whenever she wasn't sure, especially about more modern objects, she had instructions such as: "Children, draw straws for my television."

In this family, the mother placed her will in the safety deposit box, not thinking to keep another copy of funeral instructions separately. So at her sudden death, finding nothing in her home outlining her burial wishes, the family managed to obtain access to the safety deposit box, where they found the beautifully conceived and executed document.

This case illustrates the privacy that some caring parents feel they need to have to go in peace. The case also shows that a mother's concern for equity among her children becomes evident to all concerned. Even though the estate was small, each child felt included.

In traditional families, the father controlled the family finances. For many Canadian and American baby boomers, Robert Young's family in "Father Knows Best" was the archetype. "Bonanza," where the mother had disappeared and a loving, but authoritarian, father, Lorne Green, was in complete control, presented the artistic extreme. The Bradys were the "Father Knows Best" for the 1970s, giving the children of divorce a fantasy family to focus on. The "Brady Bunch" featured the wife, Carol, shopping with the maid, Alice, while the father was off to work.

While we want to avoid stereotyping sex roles in the family, baby boomers, depending upon their ages, have grown up with images of lifestyles that have long since disappeared. But these images play into the behavior of parents planning their estates. Robert Young, who changed into his smoking jacket from his suit jacket when he arrived home each night, would hardly sit down and discuss the disposition of his bank account with his three children, even though he was forthcoming on other issues. The Brady Bunch didn't bring up the topic of family finance at all.

But the baby boom generation spawned the birth of the women's movement and upheaval of the 1960s. Family roles and expectations have completely changed. So it's not surprising that the generation primarily passing on the estates is applying values that clash with those of the generation primarily receiving the estates.

A typical situation involves a taciturn father holding back financial information, which the children unsuccessfully try to elicit from time to time. One client told of walking over land that had been in the family since Confederation, trying to find out her father's plans for the place. All she could learn from this conversation was that the father hoped he could preserve a particular forty-acre lot that held much family sentimental value for the four children. Later, in a separate conversation, she learned that her father planned to leave all his money to his second wife. When the daughter suggested leaving a life estate so that the land could be preserved for his children after his second wife's death, the father clammed up. At yet another date, when his executor had a heart attack, the father admitted that he was considering changing executors.

But he wouldn't reveal who the new executor was to be. The daughter asked, "Who should we call to locate your will, then?" Stony silence was the only response.

By contrast, another family openly discussed its land. In particular, the Gibsons readily talked about their concern with keeping the family farm intact in the face of taxes. The land had been in the family for one hundred years, and the Gibsons worked together to establish plans to keep the ranching operation viable.

The older generation of Gibsons had thus openly faced the challenge together with the younger generation. Conversely, in the former, noncommunicative family, property control had always been a tightly held source of family control. The daughter remembered her eighty-five-year-old grandmother driving across her lands, pointing them out, boundary marks and all. On the topic of inheritance, the only subject that was specifically discussed was who would get the heirloom quilts.

Experiencing the death of a parent can be somewhat less traumatic if you've prepared for the financial and legal obligations you'll assume. If you are unable to talk about these questions with your parents at least familiarize yourself with the steps of the estate closure process in advance so that it all doesn't come as a mystery complicating an already difficult period of loss.

Below are some types of reactive estate receipts you may encounter or prevent.

REACTIVE ESTATE RECEIPT

CONTROL BY FAMILY MALES

Historically in families with several children, the men tend to dominate family business affairs. Although women's roles have changed in many areas of life, women still are playing financial catch-up. Women also have tended not to be as familiar with the fine points of financial strategy as men, so when the going gets tough, men tend to assume control. Even after he died, the traditional male made sure that his money was in good hands by leaving everything in trust for his wife, specifically (and intentionally) with trust departments run by men.

While attitudes about women's roles in the workplace have helped change attitudes about women's roles in the family, gender conflict is likely to emerge in times of family stress, including during the estate process.

SIBLING RIVALRY

In a family with more than one child, inheritance almost inevitably involves settling outstanding emotional issues along with settling the money, especially in families with high net worths. Money is frequently substituted for expressions of love.

Although rivalry among siblings is normal, the receipt or potential receipt of money is likely to heighten the antagonism. For example, in one family, two brothers, "John and Anthony Jones," were co-beneficiaries of a trust fund that gave them discretionary income for life, with the remainder to be distributed to their children. The older brother, John, had no children, but his younger brother, Anthony, who had two children, pressed the trust department not to distribute any income to the current generation. If the trust department followed Anthony's instructions, the trust would grow for the benefit of his children at the expense of his brother.

The Mitchells, who run a family business, have three children, Aron, Bernice, and Carol. Aron had married into a family with a business of their own and had become involved there. Carol had shown she was not management material. With her MBA, Bernice was the logical heir to the family business. Even though Carol had no realistic hope of running a successful business, she became resentful when faced with the reality that she would be cut out of active management, while Bernice would run the company.

THE SURVIVING SPOUSE

In most marriages, one spouse will predecease the other, leaving questions about how to manage the estate that's been planned together and left to one.

Facing bereavement and building a new life, sometimes after nursing the spouse through a long illness, is difficult enough. Added to that burden, dealing with financial issues can be especially intimidating to women of the older generation. Many women whose major adult years were spent in single-earner marriages will now face managing substantial estates during the period from the death of their husbands until they die. The skills for such an endeavour don't appear overnight, and these women are among the new heirs, too.

Nothing can fully prepare you for the shock of your spouse's death. Worse still, widows of entrepreneurs are often expected to rise to the challenge of taking the helm of a company or protecting the family's interest at the worst possible time. In one case, a woman was left battling with embittered business partners, each vying for control of her husband's clothing company. While fighting among themselves for managerial control, all were united on one front: attempting to undervalue the interest of the deceased partner to their mutual gain. The widow was sufficiently astute to hire a lawyer to protect her interest and finally won a drawn-out lawsuit that divided the company's assets. In another case, the widow was forced to make critical decisions about her husband's car service company left to her. Instincts eventually proved correct, but there were losses in the interim.

One way to reduce these risks is to stay informed about your spouse's business. Another is to be educated about financial matters. The requisite money management information to help you face these tasks is here in this book.

Another task may also await you as a surviving spouse: contending with middle-aged children whose own expectations often don't match their material prospects. As the older generation's savings have begun to shrink — many attributing this change to the consumption of the savings for medical needs and the expenses of longer lives — children watch their presumed inheritances dwindle.

This situation is bound to create tension between the generations. It is the job of the surviving spouse to protect herself or himself first, preserving the hard-won life savings so that funds will not run short. As pressing as the needs of the younger generation seem — whether it be university education for the grandchildren or a downpayment for a house — unless ample funds are available to the surviving spouse, he or she must be very conservative in sharing wealth. Unfortunately, the sad but true case is that the children may not have money should you need it, and worse yet, if they have it, you may not be able to count on them to share.

FAMILY BUSINESSES

When family businesses are involved, more than jealousy and bereavement can enter the picture. From the smallest companies to major financial empires, sustaining the family business after the death of the first or second generation often proves impossible.

The celebrated Canadian case of the Griffiths family and Westcoast International Communications (WIC) is a perfect example of what can go drastically wrong when proper preparation hasn't been made regarding the intergenerational transfer of wealth. Frank Griffiths, a self-made multi-millionaire and inspirational head of WIC, failed to find a suitable successor for his telecommunications empire and, as a result of his untimely death, left WIC without an effective leader. As a result of the lack of an effective and well-defined succession plan, WIC suddenly found itself divided by unusual corporate alliances, family maneuvering, and the eventual concentration of power by Griffiths' surviving spouse, Emily. This lack of corporate cohesion caused WIC to lose face as a result of family power-mongering, something public shareholders of WIC were neither used to nor willing to accept.

In another case, a manufacturing family with two children gave their son, the younger child, the important responsibility of functioning as president of the firm. The older child, the daughter, even though better educated and with a much firmer grasp of finances, essentially functioned only as her father's assistant. When the parent died, the son's lack of business savvy spelled the end of the family business.

STEP-PARENTS

With the increase in second and third marriages, a major problem facing families occurs when children come into conflict with step-parents. When the family nest egg has been built up by the original couple, one set of children is bound to feel deprived when they see their mother or father's money left to the step-parent rather than themselves. Even if the second husband or wife is only given lifetime rights to the property in the form of a life estate, children realize they may never see any inheritance if the provisions allow for discretionary use of all the funds. Depending upon medical needs or a step-parent who lives it up, children may be left nothing of either parent's assets.

PARENTAL MISTRUST

Not all children turn out according to parental expectations. From long experience the parents have learned that their children are not financially responsible. Or, in other cases, well-meaning parents create will or trust provisions that effectively limit their children's options. In either case, these arrangements reflect parental mistrust of the children they have raised. Listed below are some tools that parents have used.

Spendthrift Trusts

Spendthrift trusts are designed to limit access to children's inheritances by placing them off-limits to creditors. In this scenario, funds are left in a trust with the specific provision that no debts can be paid from the income or corpus of the trust. While the spendthrift trust provides income to the beneficiary each year, the beneficiary's creditors cannot attach the property, but can take income. The beneficiary cannot receive any more than the annual income allowance.

Silver Strings

In other cases, parents bind their children with silver strings long after their deaths. Leaving funds in trust for healthy mature adults is tantamount to keeping them as emotional and financial dependants for their lifetimes. Their message is clearly that we want you to have the money, but with conditions. These conditions include whatever the trust provides. For example, a standard of living might be specified and limited. Or, a trust might cease to distribute income if a child is engaged in certain unacceptable career choices. In extreme cases, the trust might only pay for certain items, such as education or medical expenses, leaving heirs to characterize travel cruises as "education" and personal trainers as "medical expenses."

Family Legacies

Without believing in ghosts, we can still see the effect of the dead long after their last breath. With the disposition of property, the deceased impose their values and affect lives for generations to come.[1]

Popular literature has often traced the influence of families on protagonists, and psychoanalysis has centered on conscious recognition and rejection of these influences. Who can forget Scarlett O'Hara calling for her mother years after her death, or the echoes of her father, "Land is the only thing in the world that amounts to anything ... for 'tis the only thing in this world that lasts."

When powerful figures die, those left living are often cast adrift. Suppressed feelings may surface after death, adding to the emotional confusion, especially if there was unsettled business between parent and child.

[1]Likewise, ancestors imprint their habits and mannerisms on their descendants. Distant cousins often seem first-hand mirror images of themselves.

The question of the disposition of material possessions adds fuel to the flame. When these possessions have been used as surrogates for expressed love and approval, their disposition can deeply affect the heirs.

On a *policy* level, our world is controlled by the living (for example, wills requiring marriage to inherit have been ruled as against public policy), but on an *emotional* level, reconciling the death and the disposition often challenge even the most emotionally mature.

GREAT EXPECTATIONS

A principal feature of inheritance is that there are legally no heirs until someone dies. Potential heirs only have *expectancy*. Unless the will-maker is mentally incompetent, a valid will can be changed many times. The dissonance between expectancy and actuality gives rise to many post-death traumas, not to mention celebrated court cases, most often where children are "disinherited" by an intervening third party, usually a second wife or husband, or a charity.

Remember: Generally people can dispose of their wealth however they wish. (Two exceptions are with spouses and dependent children.) Jesse Dukeminier, in the U.S. classic textbook on wills, trusts and estates, states:

> In this book we deal with people, the quick as well as the dead. There is nothing like the death of a moneyed member of the family to show persons as they really are, virtuous or conniving, generous or grasping. Many a family has been torn apart by a botched-up will. Each case is a drama in human relationships.

Ambrose Bierce — that wonderfully caustic 19th century mind — reputedly observed, "Death is not the end; there remains the litigation." While this maxim represents the exception, not the rule, recent Ontario provincial legislation provides for voluntary arbitration to head off disputes over inheritances.

Once the funeral is over and the visiting relatives have returned home, the long process of closing the deceased's affairs begins.

Although these problems are most acute in wealthy families, every heir is challenged by the pitfalls of inheritance. By recognizing the potentially damaging effects of an inheritance, you and your family are better prepared to maximize the benefits of your gifts.

STEPS TO FOLLOW WHEN A
CLOSE RELATIVE DIES

2✦

1. Determine funeral, memorial service, and burial or cremation wishes.

2. Notify the newspapers and/or call friends to let them know the details of the service and whether flowers or donations to a favourite charity are preferred by the family.

3. Establish whether burial insurance or a burial policy through a particular funeral home exists. If so, try to learn what provisions it contains before the final funeral instructions are given to the mortuary. For example, some policies pay for one type of casket but not another.

4. CPP pays a one-time death benefit to the spouse or dependent children of the deceased.

5. If there are no burial benefits or insurance, remember that someone from the family will have to pay in cash or by credit card before the final ceremony. To an already grieving family, several thousand dollars for unanticipated funeral costs can add a weighty burden, especially if travel is also involved.

6. Take time to deal with your own grief and to visit with family members, especially those that have travelled from distant locations, before addressing the details of the estate.

7. Locate the will or family trust document, especially if burial instructions are not found. But do not try to cope with all the provisions of the will before the funeral.

8. Explain to the likely heirs that the will review or reading will take place after the funeral and that copies will be provided for those under time pressure to leave.

9. Insist that an inventory be taken before any personal effects are removed from the home of the deceased. Especially where a family has jewelry and other valuable objects in the home, heirs have a tendency to snatch items that they have coveted. Or, more positively, items of sentimental significance may be carted off by grieving relatives. Bottom line: Neither behaviour is acceptable. Many items will have been enumerated in the will, and family schisms created by hasty actions during a funeral will haunt a family for years.

10. Make sure to photocopy the death certificate and put the original in a secure location. The certificate will be required for many aspects of closing the estate, from selling an automobile to obtaining forgiveness on the debts of the deceased.

11. Identify the executor or executrix (i.e., personal representative of the deceased after death), and assure that the wishes of the deceased are carried out.

12. Notify, or be sure that the executor notifies, all creditors, especially if a mortgage on family property is involved. Do not pay off credit cards and other debts from your own funds. First, beneficiaries are not responsible for such debts, and should the debts exceed the assets, the creditor must cancel the debt. Second, the estate is taxed on a deemed realization of capital property for capital gains purposes.

13. Don't expect the estate to be settled quickly. Do not commit funds you haven't yet received. For example, do not use an anticipated inheritance to purchase a home by signing a purchase contract because you might not have the required money at closing.

14. Give yourself time. Don't do anything rash in the first year after a parent's death. In one case, an heiress became engaged twice, fired all her advisors, and took over the management of her complex affairs in the year when she should have mourned her parental loss and kept a less stressful schedule.

Whatever the dynamics, pre or post-death, the point inevitably comes when the family must face the loss of a parent or one spouse the loss of the other. As Publilius Syrus said many centuries ago, "Anyone can hold the helm when the sea is calm." Your challenge — and that of your family — is to survive the transition in as calm and orderly a fashion as possible, hopefully with family goodwill intact.

3

᠅

ACCEPTING THE INHERITANCE

GETTING YOUR INHERITANCE is much more complicated than withdrawing the cash from an ATM. Rooted in tradition and law, the estate transfer process involves many legal and procedural formalities that can serve as both safeguards and obstacles for new heirs. Aside from dealing with your family, you are likely to encounter executors, accountants, lawyers, and even bankers.

Unfortunately, too many people die without making plans. *Sixty percent* of all adults die intestate. These estates transfer in accordance with intestacy law, which vary by province, and generally provide for the order of inheritance among the closest living relatives. In this instance, usually the heirs know who they are; in the extreme case, if no relatives qualify under the intestacy laws, the estate passes to the Crown. Moderate and larger estates are more likely to be distributed according to a formal estate plan prepared by the deceased. Both tax considerations and the desire to protect relatives usually drive people to make estate plans, but even loving and otherwise efficient people find it hard to formalize their own demise on paper.

First we'll discuss the usual case of intestacy, the norm for 60% of the population. Then we'll talk about the "unusual" case, the parent or relative who dies with an estate plan — wills and nonprobate transfers — in place.

The rising use of living trusts and other estate planning techniques has made probate avoidance and the elimination of its corresponding formalities, delays, and fees, more commonplace among those heirs benefiting from a comprehensive estate plan. But millions of dollars still pass through the probate process each year.

WHAT ACTUALLY HAPPENS AFTER THE FUNERAL?

Once you have dealt with the funeral, the first thing that needs to be determined, if you don't know already, is how your parent, relative or benefactor left his or her affairs. The older and richer a person is, the greater the likelihood of a will. Most people have trouble coming to grips with their own mortality and the formalities of the legal system, both out of fear and expense. So don't be surprised if your otherwise well-organized parent had a less-than-perfect estate plan.

No matter what arrangements you encounter, the brief sketch below should prepare you for what's ahead. The stresses will be reduced if you, as a new heir, understand the process you are about to go through. That process will be determined by a mix of three key factors:

• The *document or other legal framework*, such as property ownership or intestacy;

• The *size and asset composition* of the estate, which affects both the probate process and the tax position; and

• The *provincial law that governs*. For property held in more than one jurisdiction, special rules apply, and each jurisdiction has different rules.

THE USUAL CASE: INTESTACY

If your relative falls into the intestate category, you'll need to determine the provisions of your provincial law by talking to a lawyer. These provisions, called intestacy laws, will determine who will inherit. In general, one-third to one-half of the estate will go to the surviving spouse, with the rest being divided equally among the children.

When the family tree includes a child who predeceased the parent, the provinces differ in how the estate gets distributed. In some provinces, the grandchildren each share their parent's portion of the estate only (*per stirpes*). In others, the inheritance is distributed equally according to the number of surviving direct descendants of the deceased, regardless if they are children, grandchildren or great-grandchildren (*per capita*). Still other provinces follow a modification known as *per capita by each generation*.

Let's take an example to understand the distinction. (Be warned: Legal examples tend to be as confusing as the concept is complex.)

Aaron dies intestate. He had three children, Bolton, Erin, and Hugh, and five grandchildren, Chris, Dean, Fran, Ilene, and Joseph. Graphically, the family tree looks like this:

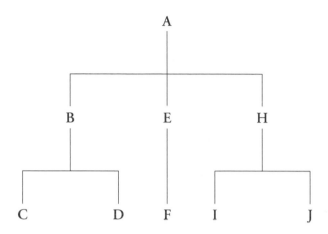

If we assume Aaron had outlived Bolton, Erin, and his wife, but everyone else was living at Aaron's death, then Chris, Dean, Fran, and Hugh would inherit Aaron's estate under intestacy statutes as follows:

	Chris	Dean	Fran	Hugh
Per capita	1/4	1/4	1/4	1/4
Per stirpes	1/6	1/6	1/3	1/3
Per capita at each generation	2/9	2/9	2/9	1/3

Where no spouse or children are living, the inheritance is determined according to a complex network of familial relations. You could be first in line to inherit from your great uncle, depending upon the laws of the province in which he lived and the number and genealogical distance between relatives still alive. Had he lived in another province you might receive nothing.

Depending on the size of the estate involved and your relation to the decedent, you may wish to retain legal counsel to determine whether or not you have a valid claim to the property. Unless you stay in touch with your family, you may not even know of a potential inheritance. The administrator must make every effort to find known heirs, but it pays to stay in touch!

A person can also voluntarily disqualify himself or herself. For example, a child may release a parent from inheritance rights by taking a gift during the parent's lifetime and signing a document that provides for such a release. Or, as far-fetched as it may seem to many of us, a person can actually *disclaim* or formally refuse to take an inheritance.

Disclaimer is typically done to avoid creditors threatening to levy or take the inheritance. Under the laws of most provinces, the intended beneficiary's children take the inheritance in the place of the disclaiming beneficiary, preventing the intended beneficiary's creditors from reaching the gift. If you are thinking about disclaiming, be aware that each province has formal requirements to an effective disclaimer, so consult a lawyer.

TIMELINES: DEADLINES TO WATCH

Although the executor is ultimately responsible for meeting the required deadlines on behalf of the estate, you should be aware of the various timelines involved in the estate transfer process.

1. Entering the will for probate: Varies province by province. Some estates are passed entirely outside of probate, other estates are held up in probate court for years.

2. Listing the estate contents: Generally, ninety days after death.

3. Federal tax return: Within six months of death.

4. Disclaimer: Nine months after death.

5. Contesting the will: Varies province by province.

THE UNUSUAL SCENARIO: SUCCESSION BY WILL

The first document you will need after a parent or relative dies is the will or living trust document. If you find a will, once it's read, a number of steps will invariably follow.

Probate

Shortly after the funeral, and within the framework provided by law, the will is normally admitted to a probate court, a special court designed to deal exclusively with estates.

The will names the *executor* (or another person in charge of carrying out the details of property disbursement) who is ultimately responsible for filing the appropriate legal paperwork. Within *ninety days* in most jurisdictions, the executor must file an inventory and appraisal of all assets with the probate court. The list must account for everything from jewelry to bank deposits.

Executors, Administrators, Personal Representatives, and Trustees

Unless you act as the executor, you will have to deal with the executor (a person appointed by a testator to carry out the directions and requests in his or her will), *administrator* (a person appointed by the court to manage the assets and liabilities of a decedent), *personal representative* (either executor or administrator), and/or *trustee* (a person appointed to control the investment and distribution of a trust) during the settlement period.

These functions can be carried out by either individuals or institutions, such as trust companies. If you do not already know the executor or the trust company's representatives, get to know them. While these people have a strict fiduciary duty to execute the terms of the will or trust, if you get on their wrong side they'll make life tougher for you. If you don't like the will, don't take your frustration out on the executor. You may need his or her help. For example, if you are out of money and the estate is likely to have adequate funds, the executor can apply to the probate court to release some funds through probate. Depending on the province, the executor can provide for the family without seeking court approval and preliminary distributions are possible if the estate is solvent.

Fees

The executor receives fees or "reasonable compensation," usually set by law.

When You Are the Executor

While it may save fees for you or another family member to serve as executor (executor fees can be waived by relative executors), remember that being in the position of executing a parent's will can be trying, adding legal deadlines to the pressures of the grieving process. In addition, the fees are taxable as income.

Your decision about taking the role of executor is not one that should be made solely on financial grounds. Executors must appear in court, and the procedure sometimes takes months or even years, depending on the size of the estate and the complexity of the legal issues involved. In addition, executors have significant fiduciary obligations to the other beneficiaries of the testator. Family tensions can get magnified when one child is accorded control over the money, even temporarily.

Of course, the process of going through papers, many of them relating to the deceased person's entire history, can be cathartic. Early childhood diaries and belongings may provide insights into a past long gone and forgotten.

Whether you have a choice in the matter is another issue. You may be named as executor without your knowledge. Your response to whether or not you are named the executor may depend on how much you like to be in control, even during an emotionally fraught time. In addition, family relationships will play a major role in determining how the executor position is filled. Typically, in a family with several children, parents pick the most "responsible" child, continuing life patterns set long ago in childhood. This choice may in turn lead to a reemergence of sibling conflicts as old childhood issues are revisited in the context of the death.

Administration

The probate court authorizes the executor or appoints an administrator to *administer* the estate. The length of the administration period varies. A complex estate with many holdings may require considerable administration, while an estate with only a few assets should require little or no administrative activity.

Administering the estate consists of gathering all the assets and debts, determining whether assets must be sold to satisfy debts, and finally distributing the estate to the heirs or beneficiaries. The first claim on the estate is to file and pay any taxes payable in respect of the terminal return of the deceased. Then the assets of the estate are used to pay funeral expenses, estate administration expenses, debts or claims against the estate, and mortgages. Under some circumstances monies can be disbursed during the probate period. For example, a widow whose assets have been frozen may ask the court for an allowance.

Not all estates are subject to administration. Studies have shown that about three-quarters of all estates skip the administration phase. In this case, the estate assets are used to pay the taxes and debts, if any, and then the estate is immediately distributed.

Terminal Tax Returns

A federal terminal tax return must be filed within six months of the date of death. Probate may extend far beyond this six-month period, particularly if the estate is complex, heirs cannot be located, or the will is contested.

Debts

Debts are generally paid from the estate at the end of the settlement process. In the meantime, the executor will contact creditors and inform them of the death. While many creditors extend grace periods of six to eight months before taking action, most won't waive their right to interest payments. If the estate has cash, it's a good idea to have the executor pay outstanding bills from the estate's cash supply before the estate is settled to avoid the interest charges.

In any case, all debts and income taxes are paid before beneficiaries receive their full distribution. In situations where debts exceed assets, the beneficiaries are *not* responsible for paying outstanding sums. The personal debts of the deceased are just that — personal. If the estate cannot cover the debts, the creditors have no further recourse. If the estate is insolvent, the claim is simply dropped, so you should not pay the estate's debts out of your own pocket.

When the family home is the main asset, being able to assume the mortgage without a new loan application and new rates also becomes an issue. Some mortgages allow the transfer of collateral to the next generation. But be forewarned: You may have to negotiate a new loan, especially if interest rates have risen significantly since the terms of the original loan were set. If the house must be sold to pay off a debt, you usually won't have to meet mortgage payments until the estate is settled. Chances are that the mortgagee will wait it out, since repayment of the loan is guaranteed and lawsuits can be costly. However, don't take chances. Be sure to check, and recheck.

Closing the Estate

The estate is expected to be closed as promptly as possible. Real and personal property must be sold, taxes must be paid, and the terminal return must be assessed. But, the court must grant a discharge before the personal representative is relieved of responsibility. Only then is the estate formally closed.

THE REALLY UNUSUAL CASES: CONTESTED WILLS

While most estates are settled according to the scenario presented above, with no illegitimate children or omitted common law spouses appearing to challenge the will or trust, the unusual cases provide grist for the media and legal mills.

The formalities required to properly execute a will allow potential heirs dissatisfied with the terms of the will to contest its validity. Three problems can raise challenges to the validity of a will during probate:

- The will is invalid because of lack of mental capacity, the exertion of undue influence on the will-maker by family, friends, or lawyers, or fraud.
- The will is improperly signed or executed, usually because of a lack of proper witnesses or witnessing ceremonies in accordance with law.
- The will has been revoked by the maker.

Will contests typically arise for one of two reasons. First, if a distributee (a relative who would receive a share of the estate under intestacy laws, such as a child) is cut out of the will, that person has a strong incentive to argue that the will is not valid. If the will was not properly signed, witnessed, or the testator did not have sufficient mental capacity to understand what he or she was doing, the will is invalid. Without a valid will, the estate is distributed according to intestacy laws, and the dissatisfied contestant becomes a happy heir.

The second likely reason for will contests is even more intriguing. During your lifetime, you can make unlimited changes to your will, as long as the formalities for valid execution are properly followed. Many people are private about their wills, and most people are consistent in their choice of beneficiaries. In some rare cases, however, neither is true. The original named beneficiaries knew about the first will, but a second will is presented for probate. Individuals named in the first will but left out of the second will are motivated to deny the second will and argue that the first will was never revoked. Oftentimes in these cases, the disappointed beneficiaries of the first will argue that a major beneficiary of the second will used his or her power and influence to cause the change. Sometimes it is a new lawyer who causes the unwitting testator to include him or her in the revised will. Other times, a live-in nurse suddenly takes the majority of what would've been the children's share.

High costs, delay, rigid formalities, and the risk of will contests have brought the probate process into disfavour. In recent years, more families have turned to will substitutes and revocable trusts as ways to avoid probate. In the next chapter, we discuss the issues confronting trust beneficiaries. Then in Part Three, we will examine the use of trusts in estate planning.

SUCCESSION BY WILL SUBSTITUTES: JOINT TENANCY AND LIFE INSURANCE

Living trusts have become the most popular and flexible form of non-probate property. We'll discuss them in detail in Chapter 4. Other nonprobate assets, including *joint tenancy* and life insurance, are also widely used to ease the estate transfer process by passing directly to the survivor or named beneficiary.

Joint Tenancy

Joint tenancy with the right of survivorship, where the survivor automatically gains ownership of the entire property upon the death of the co-owner, used to be the most popular form of probate avoidance. Then two changes occurred almost simultaneously: growth in the popularity of living trusts, which provide much more flexibility and control, and changes in the *Income Tax Act* which eliminate taxes on transfers between spouses.

Most couples hold their homes in joint tenancy, but a joint tenant cannot will his or her half to another person. In second marriages, this feature prevents a parent from leaving his or her share to children from a first marriage. Bank accounts and other assets can also be held in joint tenancy.

Another aspect of joint tenancy is that creditors cannot attach the property for debts after the joint tenant-debtor has died. Unless the creditor has moved to attach the property before the debtor dies, the creditor will have no recourse. For example, if a business goes sour and the husband dies, leaving the home in joint tenancy to the wife, the creditor has lost out. However, if the mortgagor attaches the property during the lifetime of the debtor, the joint tenancy is severed or ended and the property title converts to a tenancy in common. In this case, the property could now be attached by other creditors as well.

Life Insurance

In addition to being exempt from tax on death, life insurance passes outside of probate, directly from the insurance company to the named beneficiaries.

The Special Case of Small Estates

Not all estates are subject to probate. Provincial laws provide special exemptions from probate and administrative formalities for small estates, usually requiring only a sworn statement (affidavit) by the heirs or the executor. Forms can be presented to the bank, the Ministry of Transportation, and other agencies, and the property can be claimed or transferred.

The size of what qualifies as a "small" estate varies, depending on provincial law.

TAKE CARE OF YOURSELF

Paying bills in the interim is only one of many questions that will confront you if you suddenly find yourself as an heir. What about your own money? Time? Decisions you postponed, especially if a family member's lingering illness has preoccupied you?

Don't let the estate process keep you from attending to your own life. If you become obsessed about the details rather than paying attention to your own needs, you'll end up making the grieving process harder on yourself.

Sooner or later, the estate will be settled, and you will face a new set of challenges. Your concern should shift from the details of closing the estate to managing your new money. The next steps you make will probably be among the most important financial decisions of your life.

4

❧

BENEFITING FROM A TRUST

MOST OF US DEALING WITH inheritance will fall into the category of middle income, middle class or baby boom inheritors, for whom the expectation and experience of inheritance is a new one. But there is another class of readers, the high-end inheritors — whether baby boomers, trust-fund babies, or widows — whose fortunes are substantial and whose challenges match the size of their fortunes.

In almost every case, the fortunes of these major estates are passed in trust through the generations. Therefore, we will focus here on the special case of a trust beneficiary.

TRUST TERMS

Trusts have language and rules all their own. They are the legal expression of the control and stewardship of wealth, both materially and psychologically. A brief overview of trust terms is helpful to begin.

• *Trust*: A separate legal entity created to hold and manage property for the benefit of one or more individuals or other entities, such as charities.

• *Settlor or Benefactor*: The person who sets the trust up and provides the funds.

• *Trustee*: The trustee is the person who legally becomes the owner of the trust assets. The trustee has a fiduciary or financial duty to follow the intentions of the trust creator as set out in the will or trust instrument. Often a trust company serves as the trustee, but lawyers, family friends, and even the trust creator, in the case of a living trust, can be the trustee or a co-trustee.

A trustee's duties include administering the trust according to the trust document's provisions, in the interest of the beneficiaries; preserving the trust property; and ensuring that the trust's assets are protected.

• *Beneficiary*: The person or persons for whom the trust is created. Beneficiaries may include recipients on more than one generational level. A secondary beneficiary is second in line to benefit from the trust, a tertiary beneficiary is third in line to benefit from the trust and so on until the trust is wound up.

• *Remainderman*: The person or persons who will receive the assets of the trust when it is wound up. While charitable trusts may continue indefinitely, private trusts are limited in duration by the Rule Against Perpetuities (see below).

• *Revocable Trust*: The grantor of a revocable trust retains the right to revoke a trust or change its terms at any time. Consequently, revocable trusts, also known as "living trusts," receive no special tax treatment because no change of beneficial ownership takes place in law.

• *Irrevocable Trust*: Once created, an irrevocable trust may not be terminated by the settlor. As a result, the irrevocable trust is a separate entity for both legal and tax purposes.

• *Trust Principal or Corpus*: Both trust and tax law treat the corpus (from the Latin for "body") or principal of the trust differently from the income, or earnings, that the capital produces. In trust law, the corpus consists of the original funds plus capital gains or appreciation of the underlying amount originally placed in trust by the settlor.

• *Trust Income*: The trust income is generally the interest, dividends, and rents that the trust holdings or corpus produces. Generally if not distributed in the tax year of the trust, the income becomes part of the trust's corpus.

• *Trust Capital Gains*: While income may be disbursed to the beneficiary or trust recipient, often at the discretion of the trustees, capital gains, such as those produced by the growth in value of stocks or real estate, are not considered income for trust purposes. Usually these funds remain with the corpus, increasing the body of the trust.

• *Trust Income Tax*: In tax law, the income is taxed either to the trust or beneficiaries, at personal tax rates that range from 17% to 29% on the federal tax rate schedule. By way of exception, taxable income of an *inter vivos* trust (as opposed to a testamentary trust) is taxed at the top 29% rate.

• *The Rule Against Perpetuities*: To ensure that property did not pass indefinitely from one generation to the next forever under the control of a "dead hand," a precedent was created in a 1681 English court ruling called "the Duke of Norfolk's case," which finds its modern legal expression as follows: Any future interest must vest, if at all, within a life in being plus twenty-one years plus the gestation period (that is, nine months). In other words, even well-drafted trusts are restricted in duration to an outer limit of approximately one hundred years (assuming a trust measured by the life of a baby who lives eighty years). In practical terms, most trusts are now effectively limited by tax laws that impose a deemed realization of capital property for capital gains purposes on the 21st anniversary of the trust.

• *Charitable Trusts*: Charitable trusts can continue indefinitely, and money left to a properly registered charitable organization or institution is tax deductible on death. Assets can be gifted to an existing charity, or a charitable trust can be created. The tax break has prompted charitable and educational institutions to prepare complex estate planning packages to encourage charitable donations. The central feature of such a plan is a gift to the charity that provides for lifetime benefits to the donor, with the remainder passing to the institution.

THE REVOCABLE OR LIVING TRUST

Setting up a family *living trust* requires family trust of the personal, emotional sort. In other words, by signing the document, your parents have already sanctioned your management of their money, under certain circumstances during their lifetime, including their incapacity. Or the trust may provide for co-management between the two generations. While a key impetus for creating such trusts is eliminating the need for the probate process, a by-product is that the next generation is empowered by being drawn into their parents' affairs prior to death. Of course, a parent could set up a living trust without informing the children, but this is usually impractical. Making the children co-trustees without informing them would defeat many of the reasons for creating a trust, including the desire to provide some transition in case of incapacity.

Both probate fees and the probate process can be largely circumvented in most cases if your parents agree to place their estate in trust. However, since the settlor remains the exclusive beneficial owner of the trust property, current tax on trust income and all taxes on death will remain his or her responsibility.

Administration Under the Living Trust

The trustees will administer the trust, paying any debts that come due. Since the property has already been passed out of the donor's estate to the trust, *no probate court is involved. There are no probate delays and no probate fees*. Creditors can reach the assets of a living trust during the creator's life or even at his death. One problem with living trusts is that there is no closing, so debts can be presented by creditors in theory indefinitely. A living trust works with an estate that is fairly straight-forward. An entrepreneur with several risky business ventures wouldn't make this sort of arrangement as it might subject her heirs to creditors' claims for years to come.

Fees

The living trust may provide for fees for the trustees, but unlike probate fees, they are not set by law.

Closing the Living Trust

The timing of closing a trust carries even more significance than that of probate. The trust can close immediately after the assets are distributed. Or, the trust document could prevent beneficiaries from receiving their shares until they reach a certain age, say thirty. Some trusts may actually last a great while before being required to close. Therefore, unlike the case of intestacy, the living trust's provisions can vary widely.

IRREVOCABLE TRUSTS

In past generations, much of family wealth was tied up in irrevocable trusts. Typically, when a wealthy patriarch died, he left his fortune in trust for his spouse and children. With old family fortunes, the money was often tied up for several generations, the only restriction being a complex legal limit — the Rule Against Perpetuities (see definition, page 40). Practically speaking, a trust could continue about one hundred years, assuming one of the measuring lives lived to his or her eighties.

In the last twenty years, changing social attitudes and changing women's roles have undermined the grip of trust companies on widows' lives. Many women now earn their own money and spouses of wealthy men expect more of their money left free of trust. In the past, the husband would often leave not only his own estate, but his wife's funds as well, tied up in trust so as to "protect the little lady" from the constraints of finance. Translation: so no other man will get his hands on hubby's hard-earned money.

WHAT TO DO IF YOU ARE THE RECIPIENT OF AN IRREVOCABLE TRUST

If you find yourself at the receiving end of a trust, you'll have a number of concerns. First and foremost is the issue of what is yours and what is not. To resolve this issue, you need to understand several points about trusts. First, irrevocable trusts are a separate legal entity with a bundle of property rights. Just as a ball may be wound with several strands of different-coloured twine, the rights can be unwound and given to different people. Or, only one or two colours can be unwound, with the remaining ball later becoming the property of yet another person or entity.

In addition, irrevocable trusts have their own separate tax identity. Trust law and tax law are so closely interwoven that we cannot discuss one without the other. Even the types of trusts are defined in tax-related terms. Of all the areas of tax law, trust tax law is one of the most complex. Our goal here is to make you aware of a variety of issues that could affect you. Don't expect to become an expert by reading this chapter; do expect to be able to ask experts questions without feeling embarrassed. And don't be surprised if experts reply, "I'll have to look that up." That's the way trust tax law is. It even challenges the experts.

TRUST TYPES

Simple trusts are those that pay out all the trust income to one or more individual beneficiaries every year.

Complex trusts include those in which income can be accumulated to be paid out later, those in which corpus can be distributed currently, and those in which there are charitable beneficiaries.

Some trusts provide income until a certain point when the trust ends and the beneficiary receives the principal or corpus. Other trusts provide only a benefit for a person's lifetime, with the principal going to others designated in the document setting up the trust. Another model provides income only, but under certain circumstances, such as illness, the trustees may invade the principal.

A TRUST CHECKLIST

1. *Look at the trust document.* A surprising number of heirs fail to take the simple step of studying the trust document, or even more shockingly, fail to ask for the document in the first place. Once you are the beneficiary of a trust, you have the right to see the document. Families often try to hide the information from heirs. If you cannot obtain the document from your family lawyer with a simple phone call, hire a lawyer to make the next call for you. The trustee should also have a copy.

2. *Look at the quarterly or monthly trust report.* Without reviewing the performance of your trust, you'll be unable to judge whether the trust investments are working for your needs. If you are a life beneficiary, you want to ensure that there is adequate income flowing from the trust. If the trust is heavily invested in non-rental real estate, that works to the remainderman's advantage, as do growth stocks and other long-term growth investments.

3. *Keep informed about distributable net income.* Obtain, either directly or through your lawyer, the trust accounting income statements on which the income available to distribute (distributable net income) is calculated. Be sure that the income due you is, in fact, being paid and that amounts held back are not excessive.

4. *Negotiate trustee fees.* First look at a trustee's chart of set fees from your local trust company. If your trust is sizeable, certainly if over $1,000,000, there is room for fee adjustment. The larger the trust, the more room for negotiation.

5. *Get on good terms with the trust officers where a trust company is involved.* Trust officers are not the enemy. They are typically middle-income employees, and they take pride in managing large amounts of wealth. Of course, it is to the trust officer's benefit to manage a larger portfolio, both in terms of fees for the trust company and job esteem for the officer. Sometimes trust officers treat the money as if it were their own. (Legally it actually is the property of the trustee, but not to keep, just to hold in trust.)

6. *Get professional assistance.* Have a good lawyer on your side (not the family's lawyer; someone to represent just you). And also have a competent CA. You'll need both these people, at a minimum, in order to interpret trust documents and analyse trust practices. If you have an investment advisor or money manager, he or she can also help review the investments. But a note of caution: Be sure the particular individual is qualified in this very specialized investment area where so many legal and accounting technicalities are intertwined. Often standard investment advice is not correct in a trust context because of the tension between the needs of current and future beneficiaries.

7. *Review discretionary language.* If the irrevocable trust was set up by a settlor still living, involve that individual in the interpretation of terms such as "in the style to which she is accustomed." Trustees who are not wealthy people, sometimes are reluctant to authorize funds for lifestyles that they do not understand.

TRUSTEE DISCRETION

Whether or not trustees have discretionary control over distributing all of the income creates many issues for beneficiaries. In trusts where the income must all be paid out annually, trustee conflict with the beneficiary is usually limited. But where trustees are given discretion to judge a beneficiary's lifestyle and determine when and whether to distribute income, beneficiaries are at the mercy of these trustees. Trustees often impose their own middle-class standards on beneficiaries who may have been raised in families used to upper-class lifestyles.

Even with trusts providing for the annual distribution of income, trustees often have discretion as to whether the payments are made once a year or in quarterly or monthly amounts. Recipients usually prefer more frequent distributions to waiting an entire year to receive income.

DEFINING TRUST INCOME

Another issue is when and how trustees provide information. While some trustees are liberal with their information, others are as stingy as if the money were left for their own benefit. Most trust documents require an annual report to the beneficiaries; however, a number of issues arise with reporting.

If the income is not paid or payable by the trust's year-end, it returns to corpus. If the trustee does not provide information until after the close of the trust year, the beneficiary loses the opportunity to have an impact on when the income is accounted for and distributed. If the beneficiary does not have an interest in the corpus, then that beneficiary will forever lose the trust income not accounted for in a timely fashion.

Second, "trust income" is an accounting concept, and like any other, is subject to definition. If the trust language states "all of the annual income from the trust must be distributed to Janie," the language doesn't define what "all of the income" means. In general, trust income can be divided into two categories: income generated from the sale of assets that have appreciated, whether of stocks, bonds, and land (capital gains); and income that derives from earned interest, dividends, and rents on these assets.

The appreciation or capital gain stays in the corpus or body of the trust; the earnings, to the extent that the trust provides them, are paid to the beneficiary. Tax on capital gains on the appreciated assets and property taxes must be paid from the trust, which files its own tax return. In addition, if the trust does not distribute all the non-capital gain income, then it must also pay income tax on these amounts.

These internal obligations must be met from the gross or total income before the "income" that belongs to the beneficiary, Janie here, can be calculated. These deductions from the amount that is available include trust income taxes that must be paid on capital gains; amounts that must be held back for wasting or depleting trust assets such as mineral interests; cash reserves; money for operating expenses for land and other capital intensive investments; and income tax reserves.

The amounts left for distribution are called "distributable net income" or "DNI." You may also hear the term, "trust accounting income" or "TAI." The income which is then distributed to Janie will be taxed as Janie's income, rather than as part of the trust. Janie reports this income on her own T1 personal income tax return as trust income as reported on a T-3 slip.

TO WHOSE BENEFIT?

The question of who ultimately receives the trust corpus places current beneficiaries at odds with the remainderman, the final beneficiary of the trust assets. For example, if you are the income beneficiary but have no claim on the corpus, then you want the trust invested for income production now. (Remember, all capital gains will revert to corpus. Except for guarding against inflation by keeping the corpus base large enough to produce adequate income, there's no incentive to the life beneficiary to encourage the trustees to retain any income or to engage in growth investments that produce no income.)

The exact opposite holds true if you are the future recipient of a trust now being managed for your ultimate benefit. Your goal will be to see the trust grow as rapidly as possible. Heavy burdens are placed on trustees not to lose the money, but there is no legal requirement that they must increase the value of trusts to keep up with inflation.

Consequently, trust companies acting as trustees are notoriously conservative in their investment strategies. If you can, you'll want to encourage investments that take more than average bank-type risk. Problems occur when two or more current or potential beneficiaries have sharply contrasting goals. For example, if one sibling wants to preserve cash during his lifetime while his sister wants to preserve their substantial trusts for her own children, conflicts over the investment direction of the trust will ensue. Legally, the brother is entitled to force the trustee to invest in a reasonable amount of income producing assets, but sibling rivalry will invariably complicate matters.

CONTROLLING TRUSTS

With trusts, benefactors can control both wealth and behaviour. If a father fears that his daughter will marry an undesirable partner, he can, to some extent, prevent income from being distributed. If a mother wishes to encourage her son's future advanced education, she can provide for additional educational distributions. With the trust, the benefactor can make full use of the bundle of rights and benefits that amounts to "property." As we have seen, a trust's income can benefit one person during his or her lifetime, while the principal goes to another individual or to an educational institution or charity.

Spendthrift Trusts

These trusts, or clauses in trusts, prevent a beneficiary's creditors from attaching the trust for debts that the beneficiary incurs. Most often, parents are likely to create trusts with these provisions when children have had difficulty in managing their money. The parents purpose is usually not punitive, but preventive, the goal being to ensure that the child has adequate resources in the future when the parents are no longer around to help.

If, as a trust recipient, you find such a clause in your trust, don't be surprised.

Trust Busting

Often heirs find themselves at the mercy of trustees, especially with discretionary trusts that provide the trustees wide latitude in what income they can distribute. This dilemma has given rise to a set of lawyers specializing in "trust-busting," or finding ways either to end the trust, change trustees, or persuade existing trustees to loosen the purse strings. Good trust lawyers can comb the trust documents, the trust financial statements, the case law, and the trustee's performance records to find ways to make life more tolerable.

ROBERT NASH: A TRUST FUND BABY

At first, Robert Nash's free-flowing, curly black hair, and casual clothes hide what will soon become exceedingly obvious — Robert is the current beneficiary of a family fortune. Although Robert's usual explanation of his circumstances is long on his father's hard work and short on details about how he makes a living, do not be misled. The Nashes made their fortune in Canadian commercial real estate.

Robert's family's interest derived from owning the land for generations. The risk of development had fallen to the companies who leased the family land in the 1940s, 1950s, and 1960s, first as aircraft factories moved in, later as populations followed. Robert's family had reaped the rewards in the form of rents, which provided a steady income stream of cash to the family. Even today, with many of the real estate developments in decline, Robert's income stands at the top 1% of all taxpayers. The reason is that the developer has to carry the cost of the building and the underlying land isn't mortgaged. Although his income is atypical, many of his problems square with those of less fortunate heirs.

When Robert came to us in his new special edition Ford Explorer, he had been living his entire life off of his trust distributions. He had faced a constant struggle for control of his trust income, fighting with the trust company trustees over the direction of his investments and for disbursements of the income. Although he enjoyed travelling, Robert rarely felt able to escape. Often, whether at his home in West Vancouver, or at his Toronto condo, he found himself in conference calls about his income and investments.

Robert had been averaging about $650,000 per year in income from his $8,000,000 trust. He had steered clear of incurring any major debts and had learned to live quite comfortably within his admittedly generous budget.

As a "trust fund baby," Robert is the lifetime income beneficiary of an irrevocable trust created by his great-grandparents. After Robert's death, the benefits of the trust were to pass to Robert's children. At forty-five and still single and childless, Robert had no incentive to increase the value of the trust. Rather, for him, the size of the income was all that mattered.

If he never had any children, Robert's benefits would pass to his brother Sam's children, Brian and Debbie. Only if Robert adopted a child or had one late in life would the remainder of the trust concern him directly. The provisions would allow his own natural and adopted children to inherit the trust corpus or bulk of the capital outright upon his death.

All of these essentially unchangeable terms had been determined by Robert's great-grandfather, the settlor of the trust, at its creation many years before the current 21-year deemed realization rule.

LIFE INCOME BENEFICIARY

As an income beneficiary, Robert was only entitled to the income produced by the $8,000,000 in trust assets. In this way, his great-grandfather ensured that the capital base of the trust would be preserved to provide for his great great grandchildren as well as his great-grandchildren.

The larger the trust, the greater the potential income; therefore, inflation would lower the relative value of the corpus, thereby lowering the value of the income. But unless inflation is high, many life beneficiaries, like Robert, prefer to take their annual income and reinvest it outside of the trust. Otherwise, the after-tax capital gains only indirectly benefit Robert or any other income-only beneficiary by increasing the capital base from which the trust income is produced. By contrast, for beneficiaries entitled to corpus, capital gains are more favourable as an investment choice.

For Robert, as an income-only beneficiary, the asset allocation of the trust was crucial. Since he was not entitled to capital gains, growth of assets such as stocks would not directly benefit him. Even if the stocks held by the trust appreciated in value by ten times, such capital gains would become corpus and would be preserved for the next generation. (Of course, they would increase his earnings base, critical in inflationary periods.)

After years of contending with conservative trustees who saw their prime duty as the preservation and growth of the capital of the trust rather than the increase of Robert's income, Robert had finally wrested day-to-day investment control from the trust company. By bringing in outside advisors, he had redirected the trust investments to provide the income he desired.

When his father died, Robert was heartbroken. Robert's father loomed large in Robert's life. In addition, his father's death meant increased responsibility at a difficult time. For Robert, professional help was absolutely crucial to deal with the transition. His father's will provided Robert with $5.65 million outright in after-tax assets.

ALLOCATING HIS ASSETS

Robert had enough income from his trusts to meet current needs; therefore, he would not use any significant portion of his outright inheritance to supplement his income. We asked Robert to share his personal objectives and his preferred use of the capital so that we could help him plan an investment strategy that would match his goals. Details were not important at this stage, but his objectives needed to be understood to determine the best strategy for managing his $5.65 million in additional wealth.

Robert wanted to maintain his current lifestyle. In addition to his support of a political party, Robert now could realize another dream — to make a difference by helping children in poverty. Because he had no children (and because the trust would provide for them if he did), Robert was less concerned about increasing the $5.65 million than with helping deserving organizations.

Before making sophisticated choices about Robert's investment strategy, we needed to analyze his current asset allocation. Given the mixture of assets between trust and non-trust holdings, planning required consolidating all the assets in one overview chart, divided by type. In Robert's case, preparing this overview required persistence and detective work. After combing through tax returns, accountants' statements, deeds, and bank trust documents, we determined that his pre-inheritance asset allocation included his two homes valued at $3,000,000; two cars worth $225,000; jewelry worth $275,000; rent interests in trust valued at $2,000,000; corporate and government bonds, worth $600,000 and $400,000 respectively, and a $100,000 savings account (see Figure 4-1). With real property, personal property, real estate, bonds, and cash, Robert's funds did not appear to be especially liquid. One question we asked ourselves was what did the inheritance do to change the mix?

We used his father's estate tax return, to determine the initial asset allocation of the inheritance. The inheritance included primarily land with a market value of $3,000,000; $500,000 in government bonds; $2,000,000 worth of rental interests; and $150,000 in cash (see Figure 4-2). A review of the terminal tax return matched Robert's understanding of his father's holdings.

Figure 4.1 Robert Nash
Current Asset Allocation

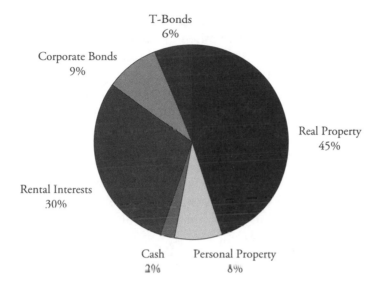

T-Bonds
6%

Corporate Bonds
9%

Real Property
45%

Rental Interests
30%

Cash
2%

Personal Property
8%

Figure 4.2 Robert Nash
Allocation of Inherited Trust

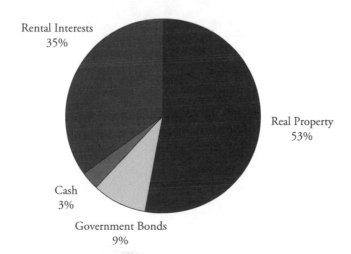

Rental Interests
35%

Real Property
53%

Cash
3%

Government Bonds
9%

Taken together, Robert's asset allocation was not well-diversified given the multimillion-dollar size of his portfolio. Prior to getting the inheritance, Robert's own portfolio was already fairly illiquid. With the addition of more real property and long-term bonds, the portfolio would be even less liquid and less diversified given its increased size.

To remedy the situation, we reallocated Robert's personal funds to improve his combined (including the trust) asset allocation. Initially, Robert did not want to sell either of his homes, but that resulted in an allocation overly weighted in real property as is seen in Figure 4-3. Using the funds from the proceeds from sale of his second home, his bonds, the inherited rental interests, and reinvesting his cash, Robert was able to develop the much more diversified portfolio shown in Figure 4-4. The new asset allocation provided more opportunities for growth with stock and venture investments while improving diversification with the inclusion of an international investment fund and various precious metals securities.

Figure 4.3 Robert Nash
Initial Diversified Asset Allocation

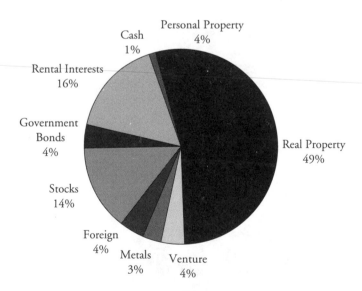

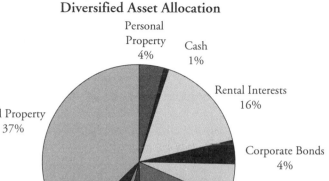

Figure 4.4 Robert Nash
Diversified Asset Allocation

As for charitable contributions, even without the keeping-up-with-the-Joneses motivation, Robert sincerely wished to help others. But Robert's social circle gave publicly and generously and he wanted to be a "player." Despite some fears that by "going public" he might be prey to less well-intentioned persons, image was important to Robert.

In order to make contributions systematically, Robert set up a contribution budget. Half of his inheritance income would be used for donations and deducted for income tax purposes. The rest of the inheritance would be used to generate income to supplement Robert's trust income and increase his asset base for the future. We also discussed the possibility of Robert setting up a charitable foundation. Although the foundation possibly represented a better long-term approach, setting up a foundation would place additional financial and administrative burdens on Robert. Like any new heir, he was better served by taking small steps, especially in the first year following his father's death, given the emotional and personal strains he was facing.

Robert decided to retain the land. He would carry out his charitable and tax obligations by investing in a mutual fund and donating to his local children's charities. Robert also became an investor in a recycling venture designed to make pavement from old tires. Robert has not lost sight of setting up a charitable foundation for the promotion of educational opportunities for underprivileged children.

Whether or not you ever expect to benefit from or create a trust, this section provides a glimpse of a different world. The privileges of wealth extend beyond having money; even the tax structure rewards wealth and serves to maintain the status quo. In other words, the rich get richer.

MRS. AVERY: A WIDOW'S STORY

While family practices and psychology vary, the typical picture in the generation now passing was of a woman who stayed at home, as a full-time mother and housewife. In that role, she often knew little or nothing of the family's finances. In extreme cases, she didn't even know how to write a cheque, much less have a chequebook. A great-aunt bragged, "I have never had to write a cheque in my life and I hope I will never have to learn how to. I left that to Ralph Senior and now Ralph Junior handles all that for me."

Like the great-aunt, Mrs. Avery's case was typical, with the added twist that several million dollars were involved. The more money involved, the more family tensions rise.

Mrs. Avery's story was almost biblical in its proportions. Her autocratic husband, Jonathan, inheritor of farm property, left the running of the house to his wife for which she had an allowance. All other matters of money were his and his alone. Jonathan Avery saw to the modernization of his 10,000-acre ancestral farmland. His older son, Perry, stayed home and worked through the years with his father. The younger son, Lewis, roamed the world on the family money, returning from time to time for family holidays, but never staying long.

When his father lay dying, Lewis returned in true prodigal fashion. He stayed through the funeral and shortly after his father was buried, began to attack the financial arrangements, which left management of the family lands in Perry's hands.

Mrs. Avery felt torn between her two sons. Her love for the son who had stayed and her longing to satisfy the restless Lewis brought her to her own sickbed. She had no knowledge of the business issues over which the brothers wrangled, and her husband's long-time lawyer told her "not to worry her pretty little head."

Lewis had done a fair amount of reading about modern agriculture, and he wanted to mortgage the farm in order to purchase state-of-the-art equipment to turn the farm from low, but steady, profit margins to higher but riskier returns. In theory, this change of income could be accomplished through quicker crop rotation and bringing into farming service currently timbered lands.

Perry, for his part, felt the pain of the "good child" who had stayed with the family business year after year, only to see his brother upset his mother on the heels of their father's death. Perry felt he knew the business and he feared that Lewis's interference would lead to the loss of the family land.

As the brothers vied for control, they also angled for their mother's disposition of her own estate. Because of past experience with Lewis's spendthrift ways, Mrs. Avery felt she should protect his future in a trust that creditors couldn't reach. Lewis lobbied hard to be treated as an adult, arguing that because he had been kept on a short string by his father his whole life, he had never learned to act responsibly or take the consequences, come what may.

Nothing in Mrs. Avery's experience had prepared her to deal with her children in the context of her considerable estate. While as a mother, she was used to the two boys' different personalities and needs, as an adult she had never had control over money and she simply could not cope with the two brothers' demands.

Mrs. Avery is not alone. An equally difficult task arises when parents, all too aware of the costs of wealth, decide to let their children learn to live by their own wits. The feeling in these families is that inheritance dilutes youthful motivation, creating more problems than it solves.

MAXIMIZE YOUR TRUST

While in the past many trusts were created to protect widows who did not know about finances or to control children's behaviour from the grave, today's trust recipient is likely either to come from a family long familiar with the sheltering of wealth or a family that has used trusts as part of an entire estate plan. If you are the beneficiary of a trust, be sure you've taken advantage of the moves in the trust checklist.

Remember, as a trust beneficiary, you are in a position to enjoy the freedom that comes with additional income. Use the time you have to become knowledgeable about your affairs, but don't become obsessed about your lack of control. You will only have limited success in changing a trust set-up because of possible tax implications. And, if you don't like the control that trusts impose, you can take care of the next generation differently when you do your own estate plan.

PART TWO

MAXIMIZING THE PRESENT

5

ॐ

MONEY MANAGEMENT

MOST PERSONAL finance books start with a quote that sounds something like this, "The starting point for financial growth, in the absence of inheritance or windfall ..."

Guess what? You are that exception. As a new heir, you need to look at personal savings, retirement planning, and asset management from a perspective different than the conventional norm.

For starters, new heirs can often avoid the slow process of accumulating savings for retirement. Rather, by following the steps below, the inheritance can be used as a capital base from which to plan for the future.

Step 1: *Budget your expenditures within your income.* In this way, you can prevent dipping into your new capital base at the expense of the future. Aside from the personal advantages of saving for your future, properly allocating your capital base also has a secondary indirect benefit: You will be providing important investment capital to maintain a healthy national economy.

Step 2: *Understand and maximize your tax position.* Your tax strategy for any significantly sized estate should be developed with the help of a professional advisor. But by understanding the basics of the *Income Tax Act* and your position in it, you'll be able to maintain control over your finances as well as interact with your advisors with confidence.

Step 3: *Plan for your retirement and your future.* By planning ahead for your retirement and allocating your assets, including the inheritance, you can avoid anxiety about your family's future while simultaneously taking advantage of the tax benefits afforded to retirement funds.

SET YOUR FINANCIAL GOALS

Although most of us would clearly like to have more money, the "What for?" is important in terms of your cash flow timing and growth needs. Consider the following:

1. Do you want to save money for your children's education?
2. Do you want to increase savings for your retirement?
3. Do you want to return to school yourself?
4. Do you want to change careers?
5. Do you want a second home?
6. Do you have a dream to travel the world?
7. Is buying a home for your parents a long-cherished hope?
8. Do you simply want to have more money in the bank?

Before taking a look at cash flow and taxes you must set financial goals. Financial objectives will enable you to put this information into a meaningful context. Think about your personal financial objectives that can be accomplished with your money: Are you more focused on your children's education, a comfortable retirement, fulfilling a lifelong dream, or charitable giving? These long-term goals will help you to plan now for your future, to budget your cash flow, and to understand your tax position. These goals will also help you to allocate your assets according to your personal liquidity, growth, and diversification needs.

MAINTAINING YOUR FINANCIAL HEALTH

Just as standard wisdom calls for a visit to the dentist and physician every year, finances need an annual checkup as well. But many people experience as much fear of reviewing their budget, taxes, and net worth as they do sitting in the dentist's chair. As a new heir you have more motivation than most to get that HP calculator smokin': Your financial position has changed. You have more to budget.

Your budget should be based on your cash flow, which is comprised of the money you bring in each year (inflows) and the money you spend (outflows). Before you consider the effect your inheritance will have on your cash flow, be sure to look at your pre-inheritance income and spending patterns. Determine whether you are meeting your expenses from income or going into debt. If you're not staying even, then you'll need to either cut spending or generate investment income from your inheritance. If you don't make a change, you'll face the constant temptation to invade your capital base.

YOU NEED TO BUDGET

Some new heirs think that because of their inheritance, savings and spending habits don't matter anymore. If you are an heir to a multimillion-dollar fortune, you may not need to worry. But most people, even most new heirs, would agree that unless you are one of the fortunate ones who don't need to consider your spending habits or your cash flow — and really even the richest do — the following discussion applies to you.

For most of us, budgeting now is important to ensure that your inheritance is properly managed for the future. Although you may face great temptation to use the money to enrich your lifestyle, by properly managing your current cash flow and your inheritance, you can take control. You can supplement your income, plan for your retirement, save for your family's future, and use your capital for social responsibility, all the while increasing your asset base and minimizing your taxes.

The importance of saving, even when a lump-sum inheritance stands before you, cannot be understated. The savings rate of the baby-boomers has been only one-third that of their parents' savings at the same age (although recent studies indicate that their parents are now spending as well). The savings rate now hovers around 4%. By limiting your spending to what you earn, you can break this pattern and help allay the economists' fear that the inheritance bonanza will be frittered away at the cost of the future.

ANALYZING YOUR CASH FLOW

Reviewing your past expenditures helps budgeting for the future. By completing Table 5 1, you will be able to estimate your monthly cash flow which will serve as a basis for your future budgets. If appropriate, you should use total family figures for income and expenses. For most items, think of what you spend monthly (such as your rent or mortgage payments) and multiply by twelve, or think of what you spend weekly (such as on food) and multiply by fifty-two. Such estimates often add up to more than what you may think you spend. In some cases that will be true, for example, if you multiply food expense by fifty-two, you will be double-counting for the two weeks that you are on vacation. Like all good accounting, these estimates are conservative, erring on the side of overstating expenses and understating income. In this way, you can create a realistic budget with a built-in cushion.

Table 5-1: Annual Cash Flow

Annual Expenditures (Cash Outflows)	Amount

1. Housing

Mortgage or rent $_____

Property taxes   _____

Homeowner's/renter's insurance   _____

Utilities (oil, gas, water, electric, cable)   _____

Maintenance costs   _____

Homeowner's association fees   _____

Home improvements   _____

Other housing costs   _____

    Subtotal, housing   _____

2. Food

Home (groceries)   _____

Restaurant   _____

Take-out/delivery   _____

    Subtotal, food   _____

3. Clothing (clothes, shoes, jewelry, etc.)

You   _____

Spouse   _____

Children   _____

Laundry and dry cleaning   _____

    Subtotal, clothing   _____

4. Transportation

Loan/lease payments   _____

Auto insurance   _____

Fuel   _____

Parking   _____

Maintenance   _____

Other transportation (tolls, fares, etc.)   _____

    Subtotal, transportation   _____

5. Medical

Medical and dental, health and
disability insurance and expenses   _____

Medicine   _____

Therapy   _____

    Subtotal, medical   _____

6. **Advisors**

    Accountant   _____

    Lawyer   _____

    Financial   _____

        Subtotal, advisors   _____

7. Phone   _____

8. Household purchases and supplies   _____

9. House cleaning and household help   _____

10. Education (tuition, books, supplies)   _____

11. Recreation/club memberships   _____

12. Personal care and improvements   _____

13. Fitness club/trainer   _____

14. Cosmetics   _____

15. Life insurance   _____

16. Contributions   _____

17. Entertainment and nightlife   _____

18. Vacation/travel   _____

19. Hobbies   _____

20. Pets   _____

21. Gifts   _____

22. Support of relatives/others   _____

23. Retirement plans (RRSPs, deferred annuities, LIRA) _____

24. Debt reduction (credit cards, student loans)   _____

25. Other expenditures   _____

        Subtotal, other expenditures (items 7-25)   _____

26. **Taxes**

    Federal income tax   _____

    Provincial and municipal   _____

    CPP, OAS and EI contributions   _____

        Subtotal, taxes   _____

27. **Savings**   _____

Total Expenditures   _____

If your cash flow is positive, you have been managing to save on your prior income. As a new heir with good money management skills, you are already on the right track toward maximizing your inheritance.

If you show a positive cash flow but you have not been consciously saving, then go back and adjust your cash flow entries to include a definite savings amount. One good budgeting trick is to do an "audit" of yourself. Watch your spending in a particular category or keep a journal of all your expenses for a week. See if your reality matches your recorded cash flow. Remember that people have a tendency to underestimate their expenditures.

If your cash flow is negative, your first temptation may be to think, "Who cares? I just got a nice, fat inheritance!" But stop right there. Budgeting is not just cash flow. Budgeting involves projecting future income and expenses in order to monitor the use of current cash flow. If you have a major inheritance and your inheritance is going to be used to supplement your income, then it should be used only to improve the future growth of your capital base. Otherwise, the benefits of your inheritance will quickly diminish over time. If you've never had a career, but have relied on family money, losing it would put you in approximately the same position as a long-term homemaker who suddenly divorces without any spousal support or financial settlement.

Remember to keep the size of your inheritance in context when budgeting. If you inherited a modest or moderate amount, limit dipping into your funds to supplement your cash flow. Rather, reduce debt (especially where you are paying high levels of interest, such as credit card debt) or fund your retirement plan. Once your assets are allocated to increase the level of your investment income, your cash inflows will increase. Then you may be able to adjust your expenditures without decreasing your capital base.

By contrast, if you did inherit a substantial amount, you can realistically consider using the inheritance to balance your personal budget. Most likely, if you've received a major inheritance, you have been enjoying some level of family support all along. But now, if you overspend — or more likely, if you invest unwisely — you will bear the responsibility for, and the impact of, your mistakes.

THE 4M FORMULA FOR BUDGETING

Budgeting should be done as a family exercise, if you are married, or personally, if you are single. Although the process of budgeting is essentially the same for everyone, your focus may vary depending on the size of your inheritance. Here are some tips:

ॐ

Modest:

Make a reasonable budget based on your past income and expenses. Do not plan to use your inheritance to make up any deficit in current spending. Rather, the inheritance should show up on your budget only under current savings and future needs, such as retirement savings and your children's educational funds.

ò€

Moderate:

Create a reasonable budget which balances income and expenses without using your inheritance. You can then allocate the inheritance between annual savings and future needs.

ò€

Major:

You can consider your inheritance in creating your budget. Best: Add a conservative projection of the income earned from your inheritance to a projection of the income you earn from work to determine your cash inflow, then budget your expenses accordingly.

ò€

Millions:

Although budgeting may now seem a worthless exercise, remember, *you can still overspend and squander your family's wealth.* A budget will ensure that your personal and investment expenses are reasonable, even for you.

BUDGETING FOR CONTROL

As one new heir warned, "The benefit of family fortune comes from controlling the flow of capital. But when you lose sight of that and your money takes control, you unhappily lose control of your life." By budgeting, planning, and taking control of your finances, you remain in the driver's seat. Simply put, budgeting is the process of thinking through your projected income and expenses to ensure that you do not overspend. With your new inheritance, it may seem unlikely you can overspend since any expenses in excess of your income can be made up by your inheritance. But if you continually cover your personal budget deficit with your inheritance, the inheritance will quickly disappear and your spending habits will be difficult to control in the future.

Unless the income from your inheritance alone provides you with enough to live on, by limiting your spending to your income, and allocating your inheritance for future growth, you will simultaneously maintain a comfortable lifestyle, invest in growth, and save for the future. If your inheritance is large enough to provide significant investment income, you may be able to simultaneously increase your capital base and supplement your old income.

Let's look at an example. Say you put 40% of a $225,000 inheritance, or $90,000 into government bonds and dividend-producing assets. If they pay an average 7% annual interest, you will have an additional $6,300 to supplement your income each year. In order to create a budget, you need to complete Table 5-2, which corresponds to the personal cash flow analysis that you developed in Table 5-1. The key component of any working budget is an analysis of the *variance*, the difference between amounts budgeted and amounts actually spent or received. You can calculate your variance each month, each quarter, or at minimum, each year.

Using this pattern, you and/or your advisors can budget your income and expenditures by month, by year, or both. Of course, the most important column is the one least used — the last. Checking the variances is the only way to measure whether you've really achieved your budgeted goals. If you have high negative variances in your expenditure categories, you are outspending your own budget. You must lower your spending in that area to stay within your budget and stay in control. If you find that you repeatedly have high variances (either positive or negative) in certain areas, you should adjust your budget to reflect reality.

Remember, your budget is a tool that is not written in stone. If your budget does not reflect your own financial situation, it is worthless. Also remember that it is a personal tool, helping you to remain in control of your financial affairs. Cheating on your budget with false information serves no purpose but to cheat yourself.

Computer programs can help you through the budgeting process and are especially useful if you want to test several different potential budgets or scenarios. But the reality is, you can achieve the same results by copying Table 5-2, using a pencil, a calculator, your receipts, and your memory.

Table 5-2: Your Personal Budget

Item	Budgeted	Spent	Variance
Annual Expenditures			
1. Housing	_____	_____	_____
2. Food	_____	_____	_____
3. Clothing (clothes, shoes, jewelry, etc.)	_____	_____	_____
4. Transportation	_____	_____	_____

			Budgeted	Spent	Variance
5.	Medical		_____	_____	_____
6.	Advisors		_____	_____	_____
7.	Phone		_____	_____	_____
8.	Household purchases and supplies		_____	_____	_____
9.	House cleaning and household help		_____	_____	_____
10.	Education (tuition, books, supplies)		_____	_____	_____
11.	Recreational/club memberships		_____	_____	_____
12.	Personal care and improvements		_____	_____	_____
13.	Fitness club/trainer		_____	_____	_____
14.	Cosmetics		_____	_____	_____
15.	Life insurance		_____	_____	_____
16.	Contributions		_____	_____	_____
17.	Entertainment and nightlife		_____	_____	_____
18.	Vacation/travel		_____	_____	_____
19.	Hobbies		_____	_____	_____
20.	Pets		_____	_____	_____
21.	Gifts		_____	_____	_____
22.	Support of relatives/others		_____	_____	_____
23.	Retirement plans (RRSPs, deferred annuities , LIRA)		_____	_____	_____
24.	Debt reduction		_____	_____	_____
25.	Other expenditures		_____	_____	_____
26.	Taxes		_____	_____	_____
27.	Savings		_____	_____	_____
Total Expenses			_____	_____	_____

Item		Budgeted	Spent	Variance
Annual Income				
1.	Employment income	_____	_____	_____
2.	Business income	_____	_____	_____
3.	Investment income	_____	_____	_____
4.	Trust income	_____	_____	_____
5.	Retirement income	_____	_____	_____
Total Income		_____	_____	_____
Balance (Income Less Expenses)		_____	_____	_____

Keep in mind that if your inheritance is large for accountants and business managers to normally keep track of your money, ask for their help in budgeting. Even moderate heirs may find seeking professional advice on a one-time basis helpful, since others can usually see what we cannot see for ourselves.

NON-LINEAR MANAGERIAL ACCOUNTING: ZERO-BASED BUDGETING

In this period of corporate downsizing and cost control, some managerial accountants and controllers, who are responsible for developing budgets in large, multidivisional corporations, have found creative ways to budget. Accountants realized that you cannot always assume that the past use of resources is the correct one. For example, just because you spent 15% of your income on clothes last year does not mean that you should do it again. To solve this problem, accountants have begun to use *zero-based budgeting* and *scenario planning* to develop budgets and projections for their corporations.

Zero-based budgeting is exactly what it sounds like: For each item in your budget, you start with a base of zero and determine the amount you should spend for each item. This process is repeated each year. Every dollar spent must be justified. As you can imagine, some division supervisors were not pleased when they found out they had to justify every dollar their corporate division received. Similarly, you may not be too pleased to justify your own phone budget when you start from scratch.

To make this process less painful, many accountants now use *modified zero-based budgeting*, which, as you might have guessed, is a combination of traditional and zero-based budgeting. This approach may best suit your needs. Rather than starting each line at zero, start each line at a minimum or base amount. Then you only need to justify to yourself any discretionary spending you plan to make in an area. For example, you might need to spend 5% of your income on clothes, but before spending more, think twice.

Scenario planning is the process of thinking creatively about different potential outcomes affecting your financial position. For a corporation like Xerox, this includes thinking about other potential industries to enter or the effect of a company such as Kodak becoming a direct competitor. For you as a new heir, this means thinking about what would happen to your financial position if interest rates double (stock and bond prices would drop), if tax rates increase (tax-advantaged investments become more attractive), or if the stock market crashes (aggressive equity portfolios could be wiped out).

UNDERSTANDING YOUR INCOME TAXES

The only thing certain about taxes, aside from their inevitability, is their incomprehensibility. Even lawmakers themselves admit the complexity of the tax system.

The *Income Tax Act* does not simply define a system for raising government revenues. It also serves to encourage certain types of activities and discourage others. Consequently, lawmakers have created extremely complex rules relating to permissible exclusions, deductions, credits, and deferrals. The intertwined economic and policy aspects of the tax structure form a constant debate as the government struggles to allocate values among competing groups while simultaneously battling the deficit.

Almost as soon as one set of tax revisions is finished, a new round of "reform" commences. But certain issues and terms in the tax system remain constant. Our purpose here is to provide you with a tax primer, a "Tax 101" for understanding our tax system. With this base of tax knowledge, you can understand the advice of your advisors, the nature of tax policy disputes, and the basic effect of investment decisions or tax law changes on your overall tax position. For specific advice, you should check with your tax accountant or stay current on *Income Tax Act* updates yourself. Of course, if you're already a tax whiz, this section will serve as a quick refresher.

The tax system is overrun by arcane terms of art or technical terms with particular meanings within the *Income Tax Act*. Canada has a *stepped, progressive tax system*, which raises *marginal tax rates* (the rate of tax on each additional dollar earned) with higher levels of income. Despite this intent, many wealthy individuals with competent tax accountants aware of the numerous *loopholes* and *deductions* in the *Income Tax Act* actually have *effective tax rates* (the percentage of total income actually paid in taxes) that fall below those of individuals with lower incomes.

In addition, the *Income Tax Act* is written to provide more incentive for saving for those with higher incomes.

In essence, we have created a "professionally regressive" tax system which rewards tax wizards and those who hire professionals. The uninitiated or uninformed are effectively penalized by not being able to take full advantage of the complexities of the *Income Tax Act*.

TAX TERMS

ITA:	The Income Tax Act
RevCan:	Revenue Canada
Income tax:	Tax paid on all taxable income earned plus 75% of net capital gains.
Tax rate:	The percentage of each taxable dollar earned that goes to the government. For example, for every taxable dollar earned at a 17% tax rate, 17¢ goes to the government. Under a stepped system, different tax rates apply to different levels of income. Under current federal rates, if you are single with $30,000 in taxable income, the first $29,590 will be taxed at 17% and the remaining $410 will be taxed at 26%.
Progressive tax:	Higher levels of income are taxed at higher rates than are lower levels of income.
Regressive tax:	Higher levels of income are taxed at lower rates.
Marginal tax rate:	The tax rate for an additional dollar of taxable income earned.
Exclusions:	Income that is not included as part of your taxable income (*i.e.*, it is not taxed).
Deductions:	Expenses that can be subtracted from your income to determine your taxable income.
Credits:	Dollar for dollar reductions of your tax liability.
Deferrals:	The portion of your tax liability that does not have to be paid until a future period. The term can refer to exclusions, deductions, credits, and/or deferrals.
Loopholes:	Legal, but often sophisticated, means of reducing your tax liability. The term covers exclusions, deductions, credits, and deferrals.
Gross income:	Income earned in any form from any source.
Net Income:	Income after subtracting certain deductions, such as RRSP/pension contributions, moving expenses, alimony paid and investment expenses. It appears on the top section of the second page of the T-1 Income Tax Return.
Taxable income:	Net income less certain other deductions (*e.g.,* losses of other years).
Non-refundable tax credits:	Annually fixed credits available to reduce federal taxes otherwise payable.
Capital gains:	Appreciation realized from capital property that had increased in value at the time of disposition.

> Only 75% of net capital gains are included as taxable income.
>
> ABIL (Allowable Business Investment Losses): Seventy-five percent of a capital loss sustained on the disposition of certain shares/debt obligations of a Qualifying Small Business Corporation (QSBC) may be deducted against any income of the taxpayer, not just capital gains.

As a new heir, your inheritance comes to you tax-free, since any taxes exigible have been paid out of your donor's estate. We will discuss taxation arising on death later when we turn to the planning of your own estate. Here we will focus exclusively on your personal income situation.

Regardless of the number of sections and loopholes in the *Income Tax Act* at any given time, the tax structure essentially allows only five ways to lower current tax payable:

1. Obtaining *exclusions* of income, which are not taxed (gifts received and certain fringe benefits from employment are excluded from tax);

2. Taking *deductions* of expenses, which reduce total income;

3. Lowering *tax rates* (by maximizing your allowable RRSP contributions in one year, you may lower your tax rate);

4. Using *non-refundable tax credits* to reduce the tax liability itself; and

5. Utilizing *deferrals* to delay the incidence of tax (income in an RRSP is deferred).

INCOME DEFINED

The first step to understanding income taxes is to comprehend the *Income Tax Act* definitions of income. In tax terms, "income" is not simply your cash inflow: "gross income means all income from whatever source derived." Certain fringe benefits, such as assigned parking, are taxed even though they aren't received in cash. Three distinct types of income are relevant in determining your income taxes: *gross income*, *net income*, and *taxable income*.

Gross income includes income from wages, salaries, interest, capital gains, partnerships, and businesses.

Net income equals your gross income minus certain *deductions*, including alimony paid and RRSP/pension contributions. Net income becomes the basis for certain other deductions, discussed below, such as the Capital Gains Deduction.

Taxable income is your net income after all allowable deductions. No matter how large your total income, you pay taxes only on your taxable income unless you are one of the unfortunate few subject to the Alternative Minimum Tax (AMT). The AMT affects high-income earners with high levels of deductions.

EXCLUSIONS

Most people think of deductions as the easiest way to reduce their tax liability, but the first place to save money on taxes is to receive income excluded from taxes altogether. If you can increase your actual income without increasing your "income" for tax purposes, you are immediately saving on taxes.

Exclusions don't appear in any of the income definitions on your tax return. Excluded income could be cash you receive from insurance proceeds or non-cash, non-taxable fringe benefits. Fringe benefits constitute a majority of the exclusions for salaried taxpayers. Within strict limits, many non-cash benefits provided to employees, such as employer-provided health insurance, are excluded from income calculations for tax purposes.

Excluded income, such as that provided by educational scholarships for tuition and fringe benefits, is actually worth more than other income. That is because excluded income is earned in non-taxed dollars, and the value of this income increases with your tax rate. For example, at a 28% marginal tax rate, if you earned an additional $1,000 in excluded income, you would gain $280 that would have otherwise been paid in taxes had there not been an exclusion for that $1,000 earned. If your marginal rate is 29%, then you would effectively gain $290 on the same $1,000.

TAXING EFFECTS

Although given for different reasons, exclusions and deductions have the same effect on your income tax liability. They only provide a proportional reduction of your tax bill. Credits, on the other hand, provide dollar-for-dollar savings. Here is a quick example of how the three work, assuming you have a 29% marginal tax rate:

Deductions

Deduction for qualified moving expenses	$10,000
Marginal tax rate	29 %
Federal income tax savings	$ 2,900

Exclusions

Life insurance proceeds received	$10,000

Marginal tax rate	29 %
Federal income tax savings	$ 2,900
Credits	
Foreign tax credit	$10,000
Federal income tax savings	$10,000

DEDUCTIONS

Depending on the type of expense or loss, deductions lower your gross income or your net income. As with exclusions, the value of deductions varies with your tax rate. At higher marginal tax rates, deductible expenses become cheaper. For example, if your marginal tax rate is 26% and your deductible business stationery costs $100, you will save $26 in tax expense. Put another way, the stationery is actually costing you $74 ($100 minus the deduction's actual value of $26 equals $74). If your marginal rate is 29%, the stationery only costs you $71.

The complexity of the *Income Tax Act* can most easily be seen by the rules surrounding deductions. Lawmakers have tried to curb abuse and limit the amount of deductions taken by taxpayers while permitting taxpayers to recognize valid expenses and losses.

Deductions are subtracted from your total or net income to determine your taxable income. See Table 5-3 for an example of the effect of deductions on your tax obligation.

CAPITAL COST ALLOWANCE (CCA): THE NON-CASH DEDUCTION

To account for the deterioration in value arising from age and use of property and equipment, *depreciation* is an allowable deduction. For tax purposes, CCA is a deduction of the cost of a tangible asset, such as real property or machinery, over its estimated useful life. CCA becomes a confusing deduction for two reasons:

1. The useful life of an asset is based on tax policy requirements that do not necessarily reflect reality (for example, an asset may be obsolete in two years, but may have a useful life for CCA purposes of five years); and

2. Taxpayers may choose to claim none, some, or all of the CCA permitted by regulation in the year.

CCA provides an important deduction for companies and entrepreneurs, enabling a continuing stream of tax benefits for investments in tangible assets and also for commercial goodwill ("eligible capital property").

REFUNDABLE TAX CREDITS

All taxpayers are entitled to a basic personal amount. This credit is an annually adjusted set deduction, indexed to inflation, which is allotted to the taxpayer. In theory, the credit is intended to reflect the cost of food, lodging, shelter, and other elements of the cost of living. At $6,456 currently, it is clear that in reality the exemption is a politically negotiated amount. To deny the affluent in high marginal tax rates from benefiting from a non-deductible credit more than a poor taxpayer with a lower marginal tax rate, the personal credit is creditable only at the 17% marginal rate of tax.

TAX RATES

In an attempt to place a larger tax burden on those with higher incomes, on the basis of the ability to pay principle, Canada has a *graduated, progressive tax system*. At rising, specified levels of taxable income, the government imposes increasingly higher tax rates. Your taxable income may be thousands of dollars less than your gross income, but the rate is still applied in incremental steps only to the taxable, not gross, income amount. The percentage of your taxable income that you pay in taxes is your *effective tax rate*.

The rate structure, along with deductions and exclusions, embodies the core of tax policy. The greater your taxable income, up to a certain point, the higher the percentage you pay in taxes.

The *marginal tax rate* is the amount of tax you would pay on the next dollar that you earn. For example, if your taxable income is at the limit of the lowest tax bracket (currently 17%), your next dollar of taxable income earned would be taxed at the rate of the next tax bracket (currently 26%). Only the new income would be taxed at the higher rate; the base amount is taxed at the old rate. That is why, unless you are in the lowest tax bracket, your effective tax rate will differ from your marginal tax rate. If we assume that some of your dollars ($29,950) are taxed at 17% and other dollars ($5,050) are taxed at 26%, then all your dollars are effectively being taxed at an average rate less than 26%. In math terms, the amount is actually ($29,950 x 17% + $5,050 x 26%) ÷ $35,000 equals $6,404.50, which is a rate of 18.30%.

Once you know your effective tax bracket and marginal tax rate, you can make quick calculations about the net value to you of additional deductions or additional income. You can also use your marginal rate to see whether a tax-favoured investment such as taxable Canadian dividend income beats a less favoured one with a higher total yield. To figure the tax increase or decrease, multiply the applicable marginal tax rate by the amount of the increase or decrease in taxable income.

CREDITS

In the constant attempt by Ottawa to use tax policy to encourage certain types of activities, no incentive is more powerful than the *tax credit*. A tax credit is an amount that is taken directly off the tax you owe. A credit reduces your tax bill dollar for dollar, whereas a deduction or exemption is only as valuable as your tax rate. Because of the effect tax credits have on reducing the total tax revenue received by the government, Ottawa is hesitant to allow them. Tax credits have been allowed for foreign taxes paid, dividend tax credits, political donations and certain investments.

DEFERRALS

Accountants like to follow the "least and latest" rule. Pay the least amount at the latest date possible. Based on the simple financial rule of the time value of money, where a dollar today is worth more than a dollar tomorrow because of the interest that could be earned on that dollar today, this strategy makes sense. In tax planning there is an additional rationale: If you defer income while you are in a high income bracket, you may be able to recognize the income when you are in a lower bracket. For example, if you deferred $10,000 that would have been taxed at 29% during peak earning years, after retirement the identical $10,000 might be taxed at 17%, and you would save $1,200 (the $2,900 tax that would be owed at 29% minus the $1,700 tax that would be owed at 17%).

THE ALTERNATIVE MINIMUM TAX

When Ottawa determined in 1986 that individuals receiving tax-sheltered income, making transfers to RRSP/pension contributions and in certain other specific situations should pay some tax, the Alternative Minimum Tax (AMT) was established. AMT is calculated at the federal rate of 17% (plus applicable provincial taxes) on "adjusted taxable income" in excess of $40,000 (subject to a limited deduction of non-refundable tax credits). Any AMT paid is deductible against future income tax paid over the 17% rate in the subsequent seven taxation years.

If your affairs are sufficiently complex to require an AMT calculation, you should have a tax professional prepare your tax return. You would need to understand the AMT impact in order to make decisions about issues such as the optimal beneficial way for you to receive a Retiring Allowance.

SPECIAL RULES

Aside from the basic rules surrounding the operation of the tax system, one area of the *Income Tax Act* that is essential to gaining a fuller understanding of the current tax system is the taxation of capital gains. As these rules are complex and convoluted, competent professional advice should be considered at all times.

CAPITAL GAINS

Seventy-five percent of the gain on the disposition (or deemed disposition in the case of a gift, emigration from Canada or death) of "capital property" is includible in income. If such disposition triggers a loss, the 75% of such loss may usually only reduce the current year's capital gains or be carried back three years or forward indefinitely against future capital gains.

RESERVES

A taxpayer is entitled to a reasonable reserve with respect to unrealized proceeds of disposition. Not less than 20% of such reserve must be recognized in income each year, excepting only that a gain on the sale of a farm or small business corporation (SBC) to the taxpayer's child/grandchild may be spread over a 10-year period. Note: A farmer may also transfer "qualified farm property" to a child/grandchild by way of gift or bequest on a tax-free rollover basis.

CAPITAL GAINS DEDUCTION

A life-time Capital Gains Deduction of $500,000 is available to a taxpayer disposing (or deemed disposing) of certain capital property that is either:

(a) shares of a small business corporation (SBC); or

(b) "qualified farm property."

CUMULATIVE NET INVESTMENT LOSS (CNIL)

Access to the lifetime $500,000 capital gains deduction may be restricted by certain investment expenses, including interest claimed by the taxpayer for tax purposes from 1988 to date. When the taxpayer's CNIL Account's accumulated balance of such expenses is in excess of investment income, it will reduce dollar for dollar the amount available for the capital gains deduction.

ALLOWABLE BUSINESS INVESTMENT LOSS (ABIL)

Certain capital losses sustained by a taxpayer with respect to the disposition of shares or debt obligation of a SBC (Small Business Corporation) may be deducted against any income of the taxpayer, not just capital gains in the year of loss. Note that the ABIL deduction must be reduced by any benefit previously claimed by the taxpayer as a Capital Gains Deduction.

PRINCIPAL RESIDENCE

Each family unit of husband, wife and children under the age of 18 is permitted to have a single family residence for tax purposes, called a Principal Residence. Any capital gain (or loss) on the disposition of a Principal Residence is exempt from tax. To avoid a Principal Residence being subject to probate on death, it may be desirable to have title to the property in joint tenancy.

BUSINESS INCOME

Being self-employed is a feature of the new economic order and entrepreneurship enjoys favourable tax treatment. Provided you start a legitimate income-producing business, even if the business does not show a profit, the taxpayer can use the business losses to offset income from other sources.

In addition, a special rule permits a limited office-in-the-home deduction. You cannot, however, use an office-in-the-home deduction to create a loss. The deduction can only be used to reduce your taxable income from a profitable business.

An advantage of being in business for yourself is that you can involve family members. If you hire your spouse and children, you can deduct their wages as a business expense and their income is taxed in their lower individual tax brackets. The only caveat is that the wages must be reasonable compensation for actual services.

PUTTING IT ALL TOGETHER

Once your long-term investment objectives are established, your cash flow is under control and you have a firm grasp on tax matters, you are ready to learn how to manage your inheritance. With an understanding of these issues, as well as the psychological aspects of inherited wealth, you have a foundation on which to allocate your assets, select advisors, and plan your estate.

6

❧

ALLOCATING YOUR ASSETS

MOST OF US DEPEND on the postal system, even though we don't have a lot of faith in it. We send postcards, birthday cards, and all-important love letters every day. But if you were asked to send $2,000 you owed to someone, would you stick it in an envelope and send it in cash? Probably not. Most of us know better than to send large amounts of cash through the mail, instead taking care to send a cheque or money order. Taking such unnecessary risks is illogical. And yet, many of us will do little to protect our entire estates. Rather than commit the investment equivalent of sending your cash through the mail, you must learn to allocate your assets. Your mix of assets must be reconstituted to reflect your prior savings and your inheritance in a new configuration.

SEVEN INVESTMENT PARAMETERS

With asset allocation, you must consider the following factors, or what we call the Seven Investment Parameters:

1. Cash Flow
2. Taxes
3. Liquidity
4. Growth
5. Risk
6. Diversification
7. Personal Preference

The multitude of relevant investment factors makes decision-making complex. Each of these investment criteria lends itself to a slightly different allocation of investments that can range from land to cash. In fact, some of the factors taken individually, such as risk and growth, lead to conflicting conclusions. No "ideal" allocation of assets exists so don't waste your time looking for a magic formula. You must weigh the importance and level of each factor. Customize your asset mix.

To ease decision making, you should approach financial decisions in terms of the Seven Investment Parameters, each briefly described here and fully explained below:

• Cash Flow

Cash flow involves the movement of your cash. You have cash inflows from investments in the form of dividends and income earned, including stock dividends, rental income, royalties, and bond interest payments.

You also have cash outflows for an investment. These include the money spent acquiring the asset, whether it be the cash you pay to acquire stocks and bonds or the cheques you write for your mortgage, and for some property investments, the payments you make to maintain or improve the property.

The expected cash flow associated with a particular investment opportunity can be used to evaluate whether investing fits well with your budget.

• Taxes

Each investment you make has potential tax consequences that can improve or hamper the expected return from the investment. Some stocks promising high annual dividends may be good for your cash flow needs but will increase your ordinary income and incur taxes at your marginal rate. On the other hand, growth stocks with no expected dividends offer the promise of capital gains of which only 75% will be includible in income.

Some investments also offer tax savings benefits in a variety of forms, including deductions, exclusions, and credits. These benefits can make some investments more attractive than they appear on their face.

• Liquidity

Liquidity refers to the ease of transferring an investment to cash. Some assets, such as a savings account, are completely liquid. Other assets, such as real estate, are illiquid because it takes a long time to convert the full value of the assets to cash.

It would be dangerous to have your entire asset base in illiquid assets. If your cash inflows did not provide a sufficient cushion, you would have difficulty getting cash quickly in an emergency situation.

You may be able to call your stockbroker and sell your stocks within a few hours, but you would be hard pressed to do the same thing with your real estate broker.

• Growth

Growth is the increase in the underlying size or original capital of an investment, as distinct from income or dividends from an investment. Some smart investments do not grow at all; rather, they offer steady long-term cash flows, such as blue chip stocks with high dividend yields.

Whether an investment increases the capital base is sometimes linked to risk, but not invariably. When investing for growth, your primary focus is on the future value of the asset. In this sense, growth is a critical parameter when investing to finance future needs.

• Risk

Simply put, risk is the potential for loss related to an investment. Although nobody wants to make unnecessarily risky investments, risk is typically thought to be correlated with growth or expected return.

No investment is risk-free; rather, risk is a matter of degree, even "low-risk" investments can be risky with changes in the marketplace or the intervention of outside events.

• Diversification

The mix of assets in your investment portfolio determines how well you are diversified. Diversified investment portfolios are assumed to be safer than nondiversified ones. The problem is that while gains offset losses, losses offset gains. In this way expected portfolio returns may be lowered. Statisticians call this averaging effect "regression to the mean."

For example, standard theory suggests that an asset base consisting only of local real estate investments is poorly diversified because the entire base is subject to loss from a downturn in that particular real estate market.

You should consider the effects of making a potential investment on the diversification of your portfolio, but keep in mind that diversifying may be costly. If you are heavily invested in highly appreciated residential property, selling it to better diversify (through the purchase of various types of assets with the sale money) would trigger a substantial tax bill for the capital gains and recapture of depreciation claimed previously for tax purposes.

• **Personal Preference**

Investors should take their personal desires and preferences into account in making investment choices. Even experienced investors regret "rational" business decisions when they go against "the gut." High sentimental value can outweigh market value and should not be ignored.

INVESTING IN A CLIMATE OF CHANGE

The chief characteristic of today's global economy is constant change. While we sleep, Japan's markets start new days, often creating a roller-coaster effect across international markets that can change your financial position overnight.

Every day new financial products compete with economically significant news for attention. Even experts are hard put to stay current. So when financial advice is given in conventional formats — with topics such as insurance, purchasing a home, or understanding the stock market — you're usually left with dated information that lacks a common thread linking a particular decision to the wider economic picture. In this shifting climate, analytical tools, rather than memorized specifics, become critical. These tools are the focus of this chapter.

In order to determine your own best asset allocation, you must understand each of the Seven Investment Parameters and how they relate to one another. Of particular importance are the relations between liquidity and cash flow, risk and growth, and risk and diversification.

THE LINK BETWEEN LIQUIDITY AND CASH FLOW

If times are tough, the first thing on your mind will be cash. You may be rich on paper, but if you can't meet current costs from your income, you need to consider liquidity and cash flow as they relate to your investments.

LIQUIDITY

Some investments are more *liquid* than others. A house is not considered very liquid since it can take months or even years to convert the real estate to its full value in cash. Investments in a start-up venture may be even less liquid. Years could elapse before the investment can produce cash. There also may be legal restrictions on the resale of your interest.

On the other hand, savings accounts and publicly traded securities are highly liquid since a trip to the bank or a call to the broker can produce cash almost instantaneously. Of course with stock you run the risk of needing your cash when the market is down.

High liquidity often involves tradeoffs. The most liquid asset, cash in your pocket, has the downside of no growth and potential loss or theft. In fact, because of inflation, cash that you hold for too long may actually lose value. A gumball machine took a penny 30 years ago; today it takes a quarter.

To be more accurate, the actual measure of liquidity of an asset is often unclear. For example, although it may take months to sell a house, there are many ways to generate cash for your ownership of the house. The ready availability of home equity loans, provided the borrower has a clean credit record, allows homeowners to get cash for their immediate needs by putting up their interest in the house as collateral. (Of course, there are risks here. You could lose your home if you can't meet the payments so we don't recommend home equity loans in general.)

Many other investments are best described as *semi-liquid*. These assets, such as short-term deposits, bonds, and notes can be converted into cash fairly quickly. Many semi-liquid investments, such as one-year term deposits, can be cashed in immediately, but you often face penalties for early withdrawal.

CASH FLOW

Unlike liquidity, the cash flow of an investment deals with the amount and timing of cash produced by the investment. For example, if you own ten shares of Bell stock, your cash flow from the stock consists of your dividends. When you sell the stock, your cash flow will include the cash you receive from the sale.

Here's an important note to remember: although both types of proceeds are part of your cash flow, you are faced with a personal challenge when managing your assets. You must segregate the dividend cash flow (income) from the sale cash flow (capital). Even though they are both technically cash, when assets are sold, you must resist the temptation of taking that cash into current income. Otherwise, you will never increase your asset base and build your personal net value.

Cash flow tends to be most important in long-term, less liquid investments because the longer funds are tied up, the more important current income becomes. For example, illiquid real estate investments producing no rent will tie up cash for years. If the investment has a negative cash flow (the rental income is less than the costs of the mortgage and maintenance) the property produces a long-term drag on your income.

Cash flow refers specifically to the cash, as opposed to the "revenue" or "net profits" (which are accounting fictions), that flows from an asset or investment during its life.

THE RELATIONSHIP

In some cases, cash flow and liquidity are directly related. A house may continually appreciate in value without producing any cash directly until it is sold. Conversely, most savings accounts accrue interest and grow in cash value continually, provided the interest is reinvested. Yet cash flow is not necessarily tied to liquidity. An illiquid venture capital investment may produce a significant cash flow, possibly in the form of quarterly dividends, whereas highly liquid stocks may rise in value without producing any cash until sold.

To determine the appropriate asset allocation for yourself, you need to first determine your annual cash needs. Your cash flow can be determined by completing Table 5-1, page 62. If you cannot do a complete analysis, a general overview of your current income and expected expenses, using Table 5-2, page 66, will be enough to guide you. From these estimates, you can determine the amount of cash you need to produce with your assets. Your required investment cash flow is the amount of current expenses that can't be met with other income.

OFFSETTING CASH FLOW UNCERTAINTY WITH LIQUIDITY

After you do your budget, you may realize that most of your planned expenses can be satisfied with your current income, but some uncertainty remains. Perhaps you're not sure if your car will last another year, or you don't know how much your Christmas bonus at work will be. If you really do think that an additional expense will be required, or you cannot reasonably (and conservatively) estimate your income within a manageable range, adjust your budget and cash flow requirements accordingly. You must be honest with yourself about your income and your expenses when determining your cash needs.

Let's say that after some budgetary soul-searching, there is still some uncertainty about whether you will need more cash. Rather than keeping more of your wealth in cash to prepare for the unlikely, it may make more financial sense to keep these emergency funds in liquid investments. For example, if you think you may need $15,000 to put towards a new car, rather than keeping the money in a savings account that only earns 3.5%, you can put that money in short-term deposits or Treasury bills (T-Bills) where you can earn up to twice the interest. When you do need the new car, you can withdraw the funds as soon as the investment matures (*i.e.*, one year from the date of deposit). If you do not need the car at that time, you can revolve the account, putting the original funds plus interest back into a new short-term deposit or T-Bill.

As obvious as this point seems, many people keep far too much cash instead of making liquid investments. Consider a more exact case. Let's say you invested $15,000 in a one-year term deposit earning an annualized rate of 6% interest on January 1. On February 16 your car dies. You can't wait until April to buy a new car, so you need to withdraw the funds before they mature on April 1. You can do this, but let's say the bank charges you a 6% penalty for early withdrawal. If you had known the car would die, it would have been wiser to place the $15,000 in a savings account earning 3.5%. But you did not know. In the absence of certainty, taking the higher interest makes sense.

How could you decide whether to take the risk? If there is a 20% chance that the old car will die, and we assume that this problem will last for a year (to make the interest rates and penalties in our hypothetical analysis easier to follow) then we must compare two calculations.

The first is the earnings we expect from putting money in the savings account, or $525 ($15,000 x 3.5%). The second is the expected earnings from the term deposit given the 100% penalty on earnings for early withdrawal and the probability of early withdrawal, or $840 ($15,000 x 7% x (100% – 20%)).

Even given the 20% chance of early withdrawal, the expected interest earned from the term deposit is higher than that of the savings account. As a result, it is financially rational for you to invest the emergency funds in the term deposit.

You also can see here why a semi-liquid investment is not normally a substitute for cash. If there were a 100% chance that a new car would be needed, the investment in a term deposit would make no sense since the money would clearly earn more in a savings account until spent.

THE TENSION BETWEEN RISK AND GROWTH

Risk and growth are usually considered to be inversely related. Although the correlation does not always come true, the theory is "no risk, no profit." Increased growth is associated with increased risk and vice versa. Because of this relationship, specialists analyse risk in an attempt to maximize returns.

The reality can be different. Sometimes a low-risk investment can prove to be a gold mine while high-risk investments often go bust. The reality is, risk cannot be predicted with certainty. However, some investments, such as oil drilling, venture capital, starting your own business, and trading in commodities are more risky than purchasing T-Bills.

THE SUBJECTIVE NATURE OF RISK

If you are risk averse and prefer to invest conservatively, you may not be willing to place a portion of your inheritance at risk in the hope of high returns. Diversification may provide you with a happy medium. As explained in the next section, diversification enables even the weak of heart to make some aggressive investment decisions without the worry that the entire inheritance is precariously at risk.

Also, risk itself is a highly personalized concept. Your preference for risk may differ greatly from your parents' or your spouse's.

Unfortunately, because risk preference is so personal, what appears to be a smart investment to you may be a horrifying possibility for your significant other or your family members.

Often disputes arise over conflicting views of the need to accept risk for growth. One side may argue that riskier investments are required to increase the asset base. They may argue that without growth, the real value of the asset base may be shrinking during inflationary periods. The other side could reason that the particular investment in question is too risky and jeopardizes the family's money. The conservatives may prefer a more conservative inflation hedge. Either side could be correct; the choices are subjective.

THE COST OF MONEY UNDER THE MATTRESS

While we're on the subject of risk and growth, it seems that the safest place to keep your cash might just be under your mattress. The truth is, it's not. Here's why:

1. The Time Value of Money: As you probably know, a dollar today is better than a dollar tomorrow. By tomorrow you will have lost the interest you could have earned had you invested the money today.

2. Opportunity Cost: Opportunity cost is the economic value given up by using resources for one use as compared to the best alternative use of that resource. The classic example is that the cost of going to business school includes not only the expenses of tuition and books, but also the money that could have been earned by a student working full-time rather than going to school. When managing your inheritance, the opportunity cost of making one investment is the cost of not making another investment with the same funds.

3. Real versus Nominal Value: One way that the government, banks, and finance teachers constantly fool people is with the *nominal rate of money*.

The *nominal value* of a dollar today, tomorrow, or next year is a dollar. The nominal value, or the value normally referred to when someone talks about a "dollar," is not adjusted for inflation. It doesn't take into account what that dollar can buy.

Aside from considering opportunity cost when investing your inheritance, you must consider the real or inflation-adjusted value of savings or investment. In 1995, it took $1.50 to buy what you could get in 1983 for $1.00.

So remember, although every dollar under your mattress is still nominally a dollar when you take it out, in real terms each dollar will actually be worth less (since R(eal) = N(ominal) − I(nflation)).

Let's consider the importance of this concept. A lot of times people will sit around complaining that they remember the days when bread was 25¢ a loaf while today it runs more than $1.50 a loaf, $2.50 for gourmet varieties. They are talking about nominal value. Market effects and wheat prices aside, according to Statistics Canada, the real value of bread in inflation-adjusted dollars from 1941 is still about 20 cents.

Also, the government often shifts statistics between real and nominal dollar values. In some inflationary years, (nominal) wages are reported as increasing while real wages are actually falling.

When investing your inheritance, you must also be aware of the real values when listening to sales pitches by money managers or financial advisors. Although your investment may earn $10,000 in twenty years, the present value of that $10,000 depends on inflation. If inflation grows at an equivalent amount as your return during the period of an investment, then in real terms, you will have gained nothing. You would not be able to buy any more than you could have before you made the investment. But at least your money will have kept pace with inflation. Such nominal growth is necessary during inflationary periods to prevent your capital base from shrinking in real terms; yet, ideally, investment growth should exceed inflationary growth.

4. Thieves: If you thought you were the only one who hid your money under the mattress or in your sock drawer, guess again. Everyone does it, so if you ever get robbed, that's the first place they'll look!

Differences of opinion about investment risk may also manifest itself in the form of silver strings when conservative parents or grand-parents leave money in a trust. One's share may be limited to income, or even only a portion of the income based on stringent or generous living standards, depending on who's tying the silver strings.

While a recipient may interpret it as a lack of faith in the benefi-ciary's management skills, these settlors are usually well-intentioned. Their creation of such a trust is meant to preserve the bulk of their intergenerational transfer for the future. By limiting you to the income of such a trust, your creditors are prevented from seizing the trust prop-erty and you are prevented from putting the entire asset base at risk (or spending the entire inheritance at once).

MEASURING RISK

Risk is an ever-changing reality. The returns associated with particular investments are often driven by a number of factors. Stock prices are sensitive to fiscal policy and market dynamics, as well as individual company performances. Real estate is typically a safe hedge against inflation, but temporary cyclical or permanent sectorial changes, like the decrease in demand for industrial property, may make such invest-ments quite speculative. Even government bonds, normally low-risk, stable investments, are subject to move with changes in interest rates or Bank of Canada policy.

How do financial analysts measure risk? Because of the difficulty involved in accurately measuring risk, the ultimate estimates are subjec-tive. The reason is largely because future interest rates must be predicted since most investments are interest rate sensitive. For example, generally when interest rates fall, stock prices fall and bond prices rise.

LIMITING RISK THROUGH DIVERSIFICATION

"Diversification is humility," said one manager of a major family for-tune. Like the quarterback who calls the play with three eligible receivers or the gambler who spreads his chips around the roulette table, a sophisticated investor will hedge his or her risk through diver-sification. Unwilling to risk the entire estate on a singular asset or investment, a combination of different investments is chosen.

As the saying goes, "Don't put all your eggs in one basket." By spreading your combined personal savings and inherited wealth across several asset types, your potential risk can be minimized while your potential returns are maximized.

Technically speaking, risk can be divided into two types: *unique* risk related to the holding of a specific asset, such as Bell Canada or Royal Bank stock; and *systematic* risk, relating to overall market performance, such as the entire stock market. Unique or unsystematic risk can be eliminated through diversification.

Diversification is also important when trying to minimize the tax consequences of investments. If your entire portfolio is represented by one highly appreciated piece of rental real estate, then you will face a huge capital gains exposure. By contrast, if you had a diversified portfolio, then you would be paying taxes over a longer, more flexible, period of time.

The advantages of even minimal diversification are outstanding. Finance experts have demonstrated that investing in 10 to 15 stocks can reduce the variability of portfolio returns by almost 50%. In other words, the loss in value of some stocks in the portfolio can be offset by the gain in value of other stocks.

This risk reduction through diversification has limits — after about 20 stocks, there are no significant reductions in risk from further diversification, but even a few stocks reduce variability by as much as 25% (see Figure 6-1).

Figure 6.1 Risk Reducation
Nonmarket (Unsystematic) Risk Reduction and
Naive Portfolio Diversification

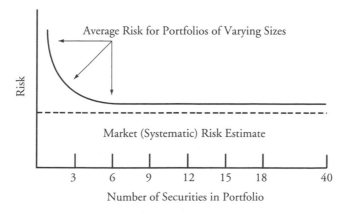

Average Risk for Portfolios of Varying Sizes

Risk

Market (Systematic) Risk Estimate

| 3 | 6 | 9 | 12 | 15 | 18 | 40 |

Number of Securities in Portfolio

Source: J.L. Evans and S.H. Archer, "Diversification and the Reduction of Dispersion: An Empirical Analysis," *Journal of Finance*, December 1988.

Money managers suggest investment in about 15 to 20 different stocks to gain the benefits of diversification. If you are unable to manage that many stocks simultaneously, you can still achieve a diversified stock portfolio by investing in a mutual fund.

These lessons about diversification from the equity market are applicable to asset allocations in the aggregate. Your inheritance can be divided among a number of assets representing a variety of investment vehicles.

4M FORMULA FOR ASSET ALLOCATION

The size of your inheritance will often determine the degree of flexibility that you have to consider when it comes to the interplay of risk, diversity, and growth. Since you will want to manage your inheritance in a single pool with your other funds (unless your marital circumstances suggest otherwise), the extent of flexibility you have in allocating your assets is determined by both your inheritance and your prior accumulation of assets. The following chart shows the probable state of the investment parameters for your combined asset portfolio. (Note: In this case, do not limit yourself to the size of your inheritance alone.)

	CASH FLOW	TAXES	LIQUIDITY	GROWTH	RISK	DIVERSIFICATION
Modest	low	some exclusions	high	low	low	limited
Moderate	medium	some exclusions	high	medium	low	limited
Major	high	exclusions deductions	low	fairly high	high or low	medium to high
Million	high	exclusions deductions	low	high potential	high or low	high

As the chart suggests, the greater the size of the asset pool available for unified management, the greater the opportunities for flexibility and growth.

ASSET TYPES

Let's review the most popular investments relative to cash flow, taxes, liquidity, growth, risk, diversification, and personal preference.

• Cash

Used by everyone, everyday, cash will represent at least a portion of your asset mix. As an asset type, cash includes more than just loose change; it includes savings accounts, chequing accounts, short-term certificates of deposit, and money market funds.

Not surprisingly, one of the most common mistakes investors make is leaving too much of their capital base in cash. Just as it doesn't make sense to leave your cash under the mattress, cash in a savings account does not offer sufficient returns compared to other liquid assets. Often, new heirs end up with too much cash in their allocations because the inheritance adds cash to an already sufficient chequing, savings, or money market account.

• Real Property

Ownership of real property (a house, land, buildings, or other real estate) is an important component of a diversified asset allocation. In particular, because of the favourable tax treatment afforded to the taxpayers' principal residence and the potential for leveraging, owning real estate has always been favoured.

Real estate enjoys favourable tax benefits for interest payments and capital gains on rental property, as well as CCA deductions. In addition, real estate tends to be a good hedge, or offset of risk, against inflation. Property values tend to appreciate during inflationary periods, which helps to preserve the real value of your capital base in inflationary times.

Oftentimes, an inheritance will involve the transfer of real estate. Although your personal preference for keeping the family's land may be an important factor in customizing your personal ideal asset allocation, you want to make sure that any inherited real property does not completely imbalance your total asset mix. If it does, sell some of the property to allow yourself to diversify your investment vehicles.

Real estate has historically appreciated over time, but the example of the recent recession affecting the real estate market demonstrates that real estate can decline in value. In addition, permanent societal changes, including changing demographics, a shift away from industrial property use, and tax law changes, bear on real estate demand.

• Personal Property

Although we like to think of our cars, toys, and clothes as investments, they usually are not. In fact, based on most of the investment factors, personal property is a poor choice: no liquidity, no tax benefits, negative cash flow, and zero or negative growth. But don't forget about personal preference. If you really want something for yourself or your family, the value to you may greatly outweigh its theoretical cost.

• Stocks (Public Equity)

The stock market affords you an opportunity to partake in the success of a publicly-traded company. The risk involved in the stock market varies greatly from stock to stock, issue to issue, and market to market. Aside from the risks inherent in the market's volatility, as was apparent during the October 1987 stock market crash, there are also risks associated with the performance of individual stocks, known as *beta* risk.

Blue chip stocks, like bank stocks, Bell Canada and Alcan, tend to be issues of large, mature, well-capitalized companies that normally appreciate slowly over time. These stocks tend to be fairly safe investments with only moderate expected returns, due primarily to the stability of the company. But as was shown in the case of IBM and Royal Trustco, these investments do not come without risk.

Small cap stocks, such as Newbridge Networks and SR Telecom, start out as issues of smaller, less capitalized companies, often with strong growth potential.

Penny stocks, that trade on over-the-counter markets (OTC) are low-cost stocks of small and mid-sized companies that tend to be risky, speculative investment opportunities, often with an equivalent chance of rapid capital gain or loss.

Because of the advantages of diversification within stock market investing, you should strongly consider *mutual funds*, especially if you only have a modest or moderate amount to invest. Mutual funds place your investment in a pool of investors' funds. The fund's money manager invests in a number of stocks or bonds, depending upon the type of fund.

Because of their recent popularity, many mutual funds have been created to target specific industries, such as banking, or areas, such as socially responsible investments. Niche funds enable you to maintain some control over your investments by choosing a fund that matches your investment criteria.

The downside of mutual funds are the commissions and fees charged by the managers of the funds. If your equity investments are modest, the advantages of diversification and money management expertise probably outweigh the costs of most mutual funds. In addition, there are many *no-load funds* that do not charge up-front fees for the investment in the funds. Be aware that some funds also charge deferred "back-end" sales charges, often for any funds withdrawn within the first six years.

If your equity investments are significant, you may want to avoid such fees by diversifying your portfolio of stocks yourself, or with the help of a personal financial advisor or money manager.

• **Venture (Private Equity)**

Venture capital is more than simply a type of investment; it is a high-pressure, high-stakes world unto its own.

The enticement of venture capital is the tremendous return on your investment.

The risks are many. It could be years before you see a dime, even if the venture proves successful. Your investments are typically limited by both legal restrictions on the resale of stock and the practical difficulty of finding buyers of such stock. Worse still, three out of four ventures fail.

Because of the high level of risk involved, venture capital investments should be limited to the discretionary portion, if any, of a large investment portfolio and only after thorough "due diligence" is conducted. (Due diligence is the process of verifying the legal and financial representations of the business.)

Despite the dangers of venture capital investing, the potential returns are not just pecuniary. Venture enables an investor to have a direct impact on the world through the flow of capital. The personal satisfaction afforded by venture capital investments is offset by the high risk and lengthy terms of the investments. Consequently, venture should only be considered for aggressive investment strategies when a sufficient discretionary portion of the inheritance remains available for such risky investments. Never invest more in venture than you are willing to lose.

FUNDS FOR EVERYONE

The marketplace of mutual funds includes varieties suitable for every investor's palate. Mutual funds are not limited to stocks. There are bond funds, currency funds, commodities funds, and international hedge funds. Funds may be general or targeted to such areas as health care, high-tech, or socially responsible investments. Funds may be focused on aggressive growth, balance, or income production. In essence, even though you do not have direct control of your money in the fund, you can choose a fund that most appropriately suits your investment needs. Among your choices are:

Aggressive Growth Funds

These funds forgo income and conservatism in the hopes of speculative gains. Aggressive growth funds are riskier than their long-term growth fund counterparts. Both types attempt to buy stock in undervalued and fast-growing companies as investments.

Income Funds

Rather than focusing on the appreciation of its capital, income funds seek to maximize current income through investments in dividend producing stocks as well as corporate and government bonds. Income funds tend to be interest-rate sensitive.

Balanced Funds

These funds seek to preserve capital by investing in a diversified mix of stocks and bonds. The mix of investments provides both income and growth.

Keep in mind that there are endless combinations of these types of funds, with differing investment strategies and goals. If the options seem overwhelming, one alternative is to choose a family of funds from a money management firm with which you feel comfortable. With a family of funds, you can easily design a portfolio of funds customized for your financial needs and modify that portfolio as necessary.

• Debt (Bonds, T-Bills, and Notes)

When you buy a bond or other debt instrument, you are essentially lending money to the issuer. Debt can be issued by companies in the form of *corporate bonds*; provincial governments in the form of *provincial bonds*; and the federal government in the form of *Federal bonds* and short-term *Treasury bills* (under six months).

Because creditors are paid before shareholders, bonds are less risky than stocks. In addition, government bonds tend to be safer than corporate bonds.

High-yield or "junk" bonds are risky investments, usually in highly leveraged companies (*i.e.*, companies bought with borrowed money secured by assets of the bought company), potentially offering high returns. Because of the level of risk involved, investment in these instruments should be limited to sophisticated investors.

Bonds are an important component of a diversified investment portfolio because they tend to be a safe hedge against inflation. In addition, unlike stocks, bonds tend to decrease in value with increases in interest rates.

• RRSPs

Strictly speaking, RRSPs are not an asset type but rather a way of holding assets. Your RRSP can contain cash, stocks, and bonds. RRSPs provide three benefits: they enjoy favourable tax deferred growth, immediate tax savings, and discourage early withdrawal (which help force you to save for the future). While technically you cannot shelter your inherited money in these tax-deferred investments which have been designed for salaried employees and business owners, if you work and have failed to fund your RRSP, you may be able to allocate some of your inheritance here. You will shelter funds from both Revenue Canada and yourself and ensure a comfortable retirement while simultaneously pursuing other, possibly more aggressive, investment objectives.

• International Investments

For the same reasons that investments in the stock markets and assets should be diversified, your asset mix may benefit from some international diversification. In this way, the domestic portfolio risk is hedged, or somewhat offset, by international investments. For example, if there is a sudden downturn in the economy which affects all domestic investments (such as real estate and the TSE) simultaneously, foreign investments may offset this risk. You might ask, if international diversification makes sense, where does this end? Good question. The best solution seems to be *international funds*, including equity, currency, and higher-risk hedge funds that invest a pool of funds in a variety of international investments. Although there are costs associated with such funds, the ease of investment and the level of diversification offset the expense compared to direct investment abroad. Other investors prefer instead to purchase foreign government bonds directly.

• Minerals and Commodities

Because of the high level of risk involved, investments in minerals and commodities, as well as investments in precious metals, normally should be limited to a small percentage of large portfolios.

Investments in gas and oil, if successful, provide steady, if variably priced, streams of royalties that could provide a handsome lifestyle. However, direct ownership of mineral rights are typically the result of significant luck or expense. In addition, mineral investments typically involve a language of their own so they should be limited to investors with an understanding of this area.

Commodities, on the other hand, can be purchased indirectly through investments on the futures exchange. These investments, which can be made on the Chicago exchange, are typically made by people or corporations with an interest in the particular commodity, such as General Motors' interest in the price of steel.

• **Metals**

Investments in gold, platinum, silver, and other metals can be made directly or indirectly by purchasing shares of mining companies or mutual funds specializing in precious metals. Although some people have personal preferences attracting them to precious metals, all metals share the risk of volatile prices sensitive to international demand as well as poor regulation and fraud, as was the case with Bre-X.

If you enjoy the glitter of gold, you might consider buying one-ounce gold coins. They are not bulky and do not require reassaying (or revaluing) each time they're sold, as does gold and silver bullion. If you do buy precious metals, hold them personally unless you've bought into a precious metals mutual fund.

Although it is not necessary for you to have assets in each of the above categories, limiting your investments to one or two categories creates unnecessary risk. Just as the athlete must be humble enough to recognize the contributions of teammates, you must have enough humility to realize that even the ideal investment has inherent risks that can be reduced through diversification.

THE MAGNIFICENT SEVEN IN ACTION

You may have already faced the investment parameters when allocating your personal assets, but when added together with your inheritance, you may find the challenge intimidating.

Take the example of "Wendy," who inherited a house and Motorola stock from her parents' estate. Because she is already self-sufficient with her $55,000 advertising salary, she doesn't immediately need a more positive cash flow.

Because she already owns a house, the addition of the inherited family home would mean that real property would comprise 75% of her asset mix. Although real estate, over time, is a strong *growth* investment, real estate presents low *liquidity*. Ideally, for better *diversification*, Wendy should sell the inherited house. Since she does not have a *personal preference* for keeping this property, she may choose to sell.

With the funds from the house, Wendy could choose to invest in bonds, a balanced mutual fund, an international growth fund, and a money market fund. While these choices both improve her portfolio's *diversification* and lower the portfolio's overall *risk*, this allocation will lose *tax* deductions that could have been taken with the real estate if rented out or leveraged for investment purposes. Nonetheless, Wendy's mix of real estate, stocks, and funds will accelerate the *growth* of her asset base through *diversification* of an otherwise long-term real estate investment portfolio.

Wendy's moves matched the asset allocation goals she had charted out using the Seven Investment Parameters. You should create a chart when defining your investment objectives similar to the one Wendy used below:

Parameter	Current Status	Goal
1. Cash flow	Sufficient ($55,000)	Maintain
2. Taxes	Deductions available	Exclusions
3. Liquidity	Low (due to real estate)	Increase
4. Growth	Moderate (long-term)	Raise short-term
5. Risk	Moderate (not diversified)	Decrease
6. Diversification	Low (75% real estate)	Increase
7. Personal preference	None	None

Her allocation of assets will also enable Wendy to supplement her current income with investment income while simultaneously increasing her capital base for the future. By understanding these and other investment concepts as they apply in the context of inheritance, Wendy is able to manage her inheritance responsibly.

Why the Market Won't Allow an Optimal Asset Allocation

It seems logical that with all of the financial experts and business schools out there, someone would have come up with the ideal asset allocation so that you don't have to worry about all of these technical financial considerations when managing your money. In reality, either *subjective* factors intervene, or the *market* adjusts to level the playing field.

Subjectively, measures of risk vary. While trying out a new restaurant may seem risky to you, someone else dives out of airplanes for fun.

As for the market adjusting, market forces of supply and demand work against predicting pricing outcomes. Thus, if you allocate your assets based on today's supply and demand, tomorrow your portfolio may be out of balance.

How does the market adjust? Let's imagine that objectively ideal levels of risk, diversification, and liquidity exist. Now, if we make the even more fantastic assumption that risk and returns for a specific asset or financial instrument can be perfectly predicted (*e.g.*, you *know* that stock "A" will appreciate 10% next month), then everyone could know exactly where to invest, right?

Wrong, because the market would not allow it. Simply put, if you knew and we knew and everyone else knew for certain that a particular stock would be worth 10% more next month, then we would all take all of our short-term investments effectively earning less than 10% this month and buy the stock.

The problem is, if we all did this, then the demand for the stock would immediately drive up its price, which would in turn lower its returns. In this way, the market prevents what financiers call arbitrage, or money machines. It is these market restraints, combined with the subjectivity of the investment factors and the uncertainty of returns, that make ideal asset allocations personal, complex, and always uncertain.

CUSTOMIZING YOUR PORTFOLIO

Your asset allocation will be determined in large part by the size of your investment pool. The allocation will also be directed by the level of risk with which you feel comfortable.

This risk preference should take your age into account. If you have a strong, stable income derived from your job that will continue for some time in the future, you may want to take a more aggressive position than if you have retired or you are starting out in your career.

MODEST INVESTMENT PORTFOLIO (UP TO $50,000)

Your primary investment focus with a modest inheritance should be to provide for your retirement and your children's education. You should create a conservative portfolio that will protect against inflation.

Figure 6-2 shows both a conservative and an aggressive asset allocation for a modest investment pool exclusive of real estate. If you don't know the market, your investments in stocks should be made in mutual funds to maximize the diversification of the portfolio. If you invest in stocks directly, try to spread your funds around a number of stocks, investing in firms you *understand*.

To the extent possible, hold cash in short-term deposits or T-Bills; money markets typically earn two to three points less. You should usually not keep more than one month's salary in your chequing or savings account.

Figure 6.2
Modest Investment Guidelines

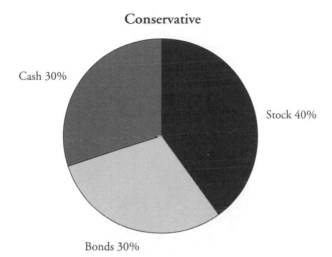

Conservative

Cash 30%

Stock 40%

Bonds 30%

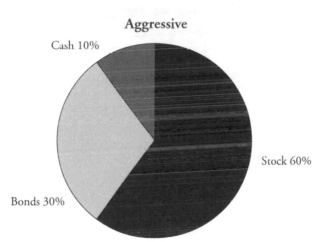

Aggressive

Cash 10%

Stock 60%

Bonds 30%

MODERATE INVESTMENT PORTFOLIO ($50,000–$250,000)

With a moderate investment pool, you should seriously consider buying a home if you have not done so already. Our legal system has always favoured property owners, and substantial tax benefits are limited to homeowners.

Figure 6-3 shows a typical portfolio for a homeowner with a conservative outlook on cash. This investor feels comfortable with over 20% of his funds in cash. Even though he is earning less than he would if the cash were in other investment vehicles, to him, the feeling of sitting on this much cash is comforting. He has moulded his portfolio to suit his personal preferences.

Figure 6.3
A Moderate Investment Allocation

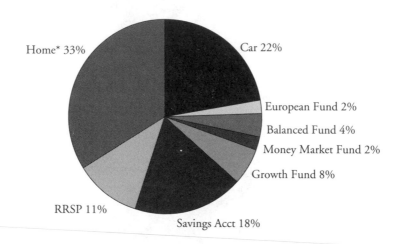

* Home estimated at $15,000, net of mortgage.

MAJOR INVESTMENT PORTFOLIO ($250,000–$1,000,000)

With a major investment portfolio, you can do more with your money. You may want to consider purchasing real estate outright or putting funds into a second home or cottage. Consider a mix of both growth small-cap stocks and dividend-producing large cap stocks. To ease this process, you could invest in a family of mutual funds providing both growth and income-oriented equity funds. Figure 6-4 shows how the real estate investments could affect your asset mix. If you are at the high-end of the investment scale, you may consider approaching the more diversified asset allocations shown in Exhibit 6-5.

Figure 6.4
Major Investment Guidelines

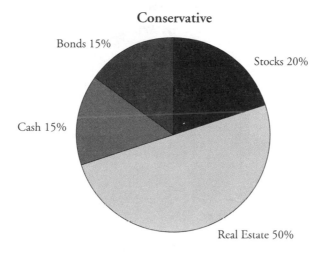

Conservative

Bonds 15%

Stocks 20%

Cash 15%

Real Estate 50%

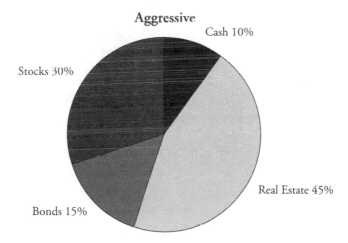

Aggressive

Cash 10%

Stocks 30%

Real Estate 45%

Bonds 15%

MULTIMILLION-DOLLAR INVESTMENT PORTFOLIO
(OVER $1,000,000)

Figure 6-5 shows more diversified asset allocations that are typical for conservative and aggressive investors with enough money to play different parts of the investment universe. With such a large investment pool,

Figure 6.5
More Diversified Investment Guidelines

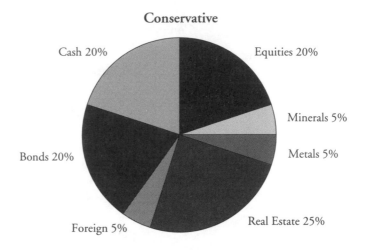

Conservative

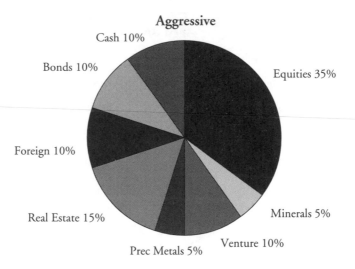

Aggressive

Note: This guide is fact dependent, subject to your individual needs and
market conditions.

even the conservative investor can add metals, minerals, and international investments to the portfolio. Aggressive investors may also want
to invest in an interesting and viable new business venture.

Although these charts provide a framework for thinking about your
own asset allocations, remember that *every allocation must be customized*

for the individual. You also need to consider your own investment objectives and investment criteria. By diversifying, you can more comfortably place a portion of your assets in higher-risk investments, satisfy your liquidity needs, and maximize your returns while minimizing the total risk of your investments.

USING YOUR FINANCIAL KNOWLEDGE

The importance of diversifying your assets cannot be overstated, especially in light of the risk, growth, and liquidity concepts discussed above. By being overly conservative and holding too large a proportion of your wealth in cash (much like the pioneers who hid their family fortunes under their mattresses), your asset base will stagnate, potentially declining in real terms, and socially responsible investment opportunities may be missed. By staying too attached to your settlor's past, you may place your family's future at the mercy of an unpredictable market that offers low returns or demands the absorption of too much risk. By over-relying on an "unbeatable" real estate opportunity, you could dangerously limit liquidity in investments that could suddenly become extremely risky, as was the case for many family fortunes in the early 1990s. Each of these potentially damaging investment biases are exhibited by the stories of Sarah Hendon, Michele Greene, James Joseph, and George Alexander whom we will meet in the next chapter.

Everyone is susceptible to making poor investments. Even the top analysts have lost as the market or the economy takes unexpected turns. Avoid the risks, costs, and dangers that you can control because there is no sure safe and quick way to increase your assets and produce income. As illustrated by the cases in the next chapter, proper planning and asset allocation can go far in properly managing your inheritance for yourself and the future.

7

CASE STUDIES IN ASSET ALLOCATION

EACH INHERITANCE SITUATION requires particular advice, but the general lessons of managing an inheritance apply to all heirs, no matter what their family background may be. In each of the four cases that follow, we focus on distinctive issues that may arise when combining the lump-sum receipt of an inheritance with your own portfolio accumulated over a period of years.

Sarah Hendon, Michele Greene, James Joseph, and George Alexander illustrate that inheriting money requires an active approach. Conserving the new assets while merging them into the existing financial holdings requires careful attention and finesse.

Sarah Hendon, a *major* heir, typifies the danger of new heirs being overly sentimental about family investments. For Sarah, refusal to diversify placed her inheritance at risk, and she used the fear of paying additional taxes as a shield to hide from the facts — she was unable to let go of her father's hard-earned stocks.

Bookstore-owner Michele Greene, a *moderate* heir, faces a different challenge. Her share of a co-owned bookstore netted her $60,000 a year, but produced few growth prospects due to the changing nature of independent store ownership. When her mother's estate was settled, Michele's $100,000 share produced her first real opportunity to invest in a growth-oriented portfolio for future security. But like many small-business owners, Michele had concentrated her attention on her business. She had never enjoyed the luxury of exploring investment strategies. The inheritance has afforded the opportunity to build a balanced portfolio from scratch, but Michele doesn't know where to start.

James Joseph, a *modest* heir, stands as a warning to the uninformed: The temptations of a lump-sum inheritance are great. He and his wife had squandered most of their inheritance, one that could have provided for his lifestyle and children for years to come, in just a couple of months. Now the potential value of the inheritance is essentially lost, since his yearly income is not able to replace it, and his story remains as a lesson in responsibility.

George Alexander, a *millionaire* heir, reveals the complications facing even sophisticated inheritors. George has inherited both personal and business assets, all of which require his attention. The complexity of his business hid an unbalanced overall asset allocation. The redistribution of his wealth enabled him to meet his cash flow and liquidity requirements while achieving both higher growth and returns.

Typical problems and biases facing new heirs loom large in these cases. By looking at their actions, you can begin to recognize your own challenges and work toward a more balanced approach.

SARAH HENDON: TIED TO THE PAST

Like many of her contemporaries, Dr. Sarah Hendon gained her position through persistence and hard work. Sarah's success began in 1961, when she received a scholarship to attend the University of British Columbia to study biology. Nine years later, after changing her major twice, Sarah graduated with a Ph.D. in child psychology. All this while her father worked at Seagram, with his employee stock options constantly rising.

Even though she faced the dual challenges of being a single mother and a professional, Sarah had been self-sufficient for several years now. She had filed for divorce after eighteen years of marriage to Denzel and had retained custody of her sixteen-year-old daughter, Caryn. From her $75,000 annual take-home from her practice, Sarah had built a $65,000 asset base. Her treasure chest included her town house with $30,000 in equity; a Jeep Cherokee 4x4 and assorted furniture worth about $12,000; $15,000 in money market funds (including Caryn's RESP fund); and an $8,000 RRSP.

Despite the coolness of her beige suit against her dark skin, the tension inside was apparent when she entered our office. When her father had passed away several months earlier, he had willed Sarah his corporate holdings. When she received them, the stocks had a market value of $225,000, representing the majority of her inheritance of $275,000. She was proud to be the recipient of the stock of the company that had been so good to her family. Yet, over the last few nights, she had not been able to sleep as stock market trading had become volatile, and Sarah sought our advice. Once we generated a chart of

Figure 7.1 Sarah Hendon
Initial Asset Allocation

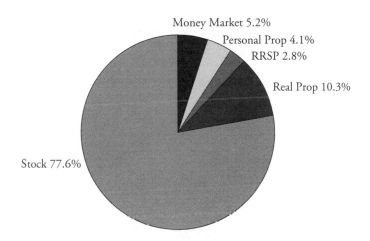

Inheritance: $275,000

Sarah's asset allocation, her lopsided investment portfolio was thrown into bold relief (see Figure 7-1).

Her stock at 77.6% ran far too high; real estate, 10.3%; money market, 5.2%; personal property, 4.1%; and an RRSP, 2.8%. Just glancing at the chart shows how lopsided the investments were.

Regardless of Sarah's other assets, the addition of the inherited stock gave her an extremely undiversified total asset allocation. With over three-quarters (77%) of Sarah's total assets in a single stock and the remainder of her more diversified holdings representing less than one-quarter of the pie, Sarah placed her financial health at unnecessary risk. If the stock market fell by a substantial amount, as it did in October 1987, her inheritance could be reduced by as much as one-third. This kind of risk is known as systematic risk, or risk from changes in the market as a whole.

Although converting some of the stock into other assets obviously made financial sense, Sarah hesitated. She admitted her sentimental attachment to the stock.

As a rationale for not selling, Sarah cited her concern about taxes on capital gains. But, as we showed Sarah, this point was irrelevant.

Heirs receive a *stepped-up basis* in stocks they inherit. The estate values the stock at its market value on the date of death. The estate then pays taxes on the stock at this appreciated value. The inheritor then receives the stock with a new, stepped-up basis (at the appreciated value on the date of death).

So, even though the stock may have appreciated since it was originally purchased, taxable capital gains would include only increases in the value of the stock above its value at the date of her father's death, not from the time her father acquired the stock. In other words, if Sarah's father had purchased the stock at $4, the stock had a market value of $9 on the date of his death, and Sarah sold the stock at $10, the tax would be on the capital gain of $1 (the difference between the $10 sales price and Sarah's $9 stepped-up basis, as compared to the $6 in capital gains that she would have been taxed on had her father given her the stock during his lifetime). The capital gains tax liability that Sarah faced was consequently much lower than she had feared.

Sarah needed diversification. The balanced mix of different types of assets or investments is especially important in properly managing an inheritance because the addition of someone else's portfolio to your own inevitably creates a different mix.

If her assets were a banana cream pie, and the huge stock slice were accidentally knocked on the floor, Sarah would never get to enjoy most of the pie. Sarah saw that it would be better to face the possibility of losing one or two small slices than one big chunk.

Similarly, financial analysts have learned that the increase in the number of stocks held in an equity portfolio from one to ten will reduce systematic risk by more than 25%. By holding more than one stock, the risk associated with the holding of any one stock is reduced. This same logic is followed by anyone who keeps more than one set of keys to reduce the consequences of losing any one set.

After our explanation, Sarah agreed to a staged conversion of the stock, selling a total of half of her corporate stock. That portion would then be converted to achieve the more diversified asset allocation shown in Figure 7-2. At 38%, the proportion of equities was still quite high; but Sarah's personal preference for the corporate stock, rooted in sentimentality about her father's lifework, put the exception within tolerable limits.

In addition, as seen in Figure 7-2, Sarah added to her real property by making a down payment on a piece of land next to her house, bringing the real estate total to 20%. She also entered other new markets in a

Figure 7.2 Sarah Hendon
Managed Asset Allocation

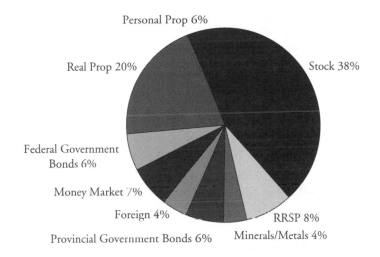

Personal Prop 6%

Real Prop 20%

Stock 38%

Federal Government
Bonds 6%

Money Market 7%

Foreign 4%

Provincial Government Bonds 6%

Minerals/Metals 4%

RRSP 8%

Moderate Inheritance: $275,000
Aggressive Long-Term Growth Portfolio

modest way, allocating 6% to federal government bonds, 6% to provincial government bonds, 4% to a foreign bond fund, and 4% to precious metals, in her case, in one-ounce gold Canadian "maple-leaf" coins.

Once her capital base has grown, Sarah intends to set a small portion aside for venture opportunities. Her dream: to provide capital for a specialty shop selling crafts and children's toys. This riskier venture investment was not yet practical for Sarah with her limited assets. Later, when she could afford to be aggressive with a portion of her capital base (and stand the risk of loss), such an investment opportunity would be possible through the flow of her capital.

In a more typical, conservative asset allocation, only about 20% to 30% of her assets would be held in equities, but as Sarah's case illustrates, new heirs should not completely discount their personal preferences. The satisfaction, or as economists call it, "utility," derived from following personal preferences does have actual value although it is often difficult to measure. If you try to deny your preferences, you'll cause yourself emotional turmoil that may not outweigh the risk in question.

MICHELE GREENE: INVESTING WITHOUT EXPERIENCE

Michele Greene has learned to live comfortably in her one-bedroom apartment in Toronto. She spends most of her day at her trendy downtown bookstore with her partner Lauren. Over the last ten years, Michele has been designing jewelry in her free time. Four years ago, she began to display the jewelry in the store and has continued to sell a small but steady amount. Her long bookstore hours combined with her jewelry sales together netted her about $60,000 per year. Since she lives in a rent-controlled apartment, Michele's income was adequate to keep her enjoying life in the expensive city.

Most of Michele's income has been consumed on food, clothes, and satisfying her love for dance. At forty-two, she has long since learned to live happily as a single, curling up alone with a book or attending dance performances. She had always loved the pace of urban life. But the last four months have been difficult for Michele. She lost one of her best friends in the world, her mother.

When her father passed away three years earlier, Michele became even closer to her mother than before. Michele had handled the closing of his estate, so she knew that at her mother's death, the remainder of her parents' assets would be divided between her and her sister. Her mother's executor, their family lawyer, confirmed the arrangements. When the sale of her parents' house was complete and the taxes paid by the estate, Michele and her sister would each receive about $100,000 in cash. At the time, the inheritance seemed little comfort to the emotional loss of her mom, but as the months passed, Michele realized that she needed to prepare for managing her inheritance.

When we first met Michele, she leaned towards putting most of the money into her bookstore. She felt it would provide a good cushion for the operation and would enable her to "relieve some stress" by taking the edge off of the operation's carefully managed cash flow.

Although the store provided Michele with a comfortable, steady income, there was little opportunity for growth given the proliferation of large, corporate bookstores throughout the city. Even if the store were sold, a financial windfall for Michele seemed unlikely, given the competition, the store's modest revenue stream, and her partnership with Lauren. Infusing additional working capital would do little to change this picture. Lauren had no equivalent amount to invest, so for minimum gains in operational cash flow, Michele would lose the chance to increase her inheritance.

Instead, if she pursued a medium-growth, long-term investment strategy, Michele could increase her inherited capital base while maintaining her current lifestyle on her current income. If she later desired to pursue a different lifestyle, she would be able to use the investment income from the future, larger capital base. Given her current needs and interests, as well as the enjoyment she receives from her work, there was no reason for Michele to change her lifestyle or to risk her inheritance on the bookstore.

Turning to the issue of investments, Michele argued for keeping the inheritance in her savings account. But while this strategy made some sense for her, given her modest savings account, a significant portion of Michele's wealth would be underinvested if the inheritance were not better allocated.

Michele's chief concern turned on the issue of safety. She wanted to bolster her savings account and have cash on hand in case of a problem with the bookstore. To her, preserving the $100,000 intact in a savings account was more important than increasing her risk. However, Michele was forgetting about inflation. Earning 2.5% compared to inflation of 3.5%, money in her savings account would actually decline in real value. By selecting virtually risk-free medium-term triple "A" bonds, her earnings could double the yield of her savings account without significantly increasing her risk. Of course, Michele would want to diversify her portfolio because if inflation really heated up, even these government bonds would not be that safe. Remember, in an inflationary climate, the income from the bonds is fixed, but the real value of that interest income declines because of inflation. As a result, the prices of the bonds you hold drop.

With our help, Michele developed a diversified portfolio of moderate risk assets (see Figure 7-3) which emphasized moderate long-term growth and minimal total risk. Michele allocated $10,000 in large cap stocks which are mostly safe, blue chip stocks. She placed another $10,000 in an aggressive growth equity fund. The fund's investments were in more aggressive small cap stocks from small and mid-sized companies. (Usually with the smaller capitalizations there is greater risk, but the potential of greater growth, than with larger, more heavily capitalized companies.) These equity investments, with varying risks and returns, offer the potential for growth of the capital base. Also, some of the stocks provide dividend income that could be reinvested or could supplement Michele's income.

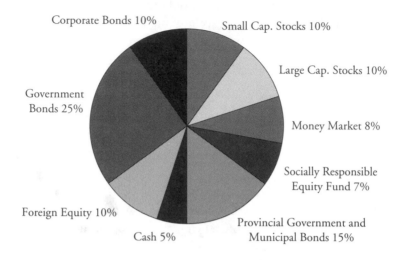

**Figure 7.3 Michele Greene
Planned Asset Allocation**

Corporate Bonds 10%

Small Cap. Stocks 10%

Large Cap. Stocks 10%

Government
Bonds 25%

Money Market 8%

Socially Responsible
Equity Fund 7%

Foreign Equity 10%

Provincial Government and
Municipal Bonds 15%

Cash 5%

**Moderate Inheritance: $100,000
Long-Term-Growth Oriented Portfolio**

Corporate bonds were purchased for $10,000; quality bonds and other government debt instruments accounted for another $25,000; and $15,000 was invested in a bond fund. Such bond funds provide modest yields and safely diversify income.

Financial analysts have recently broadened the concept of diversification to the global scale. Not only should assets be diversified between national markets, but national markets should be somewhat balanced with international markets. In this way, risks related to the Canadian economy can be partially offset by the performance of international markets, such as the European Common Market or the U.S. market. To complete the diversification process and add international components, another $10,000 went to a European Growth Fund.

Michele decided to use the remainder of the inheritance, outside of $13,000 held in cash and money-market accounts, for socially responsible investing. Although the term was new, the concept was not. Michele wanted to direct her investments, or her donations, to make a difference. Once she was introduced to the world of "socially responsible investing," Michele was ready to explore the equity and other investment funds that had been created to consider a company's qualitative contributions to society along with its quantitative returns. She also considered joining an investment group set up to invest capital in socially responsible ventures. As a starter, $7,000 went into a socially responsible growth fund.

With this asset allocation plan, Michele met her goals of maintaining her current comfortable lifestyle while expanding her capital base for the future.

JAMES JOSEPH: LOSING FOR THE MOMENT

At thirty-four, James Joseph received an unexpected letter from the executor of his uncle's estate, notifying him that he was his uncle's sole heir.

James worked as a senior manager in the marketing department of a general insurer. With his $54,000 salary he had been hard-pressed to provide for his daughters Randy, three, and Ashton, six, even given the help of his wife Kim's $10,000 earnings as a part-time decorator.

In April, James received this unanticipated inheritance from his uncle's estate, a cheque for $125,000. While he knew that his uncle had always worked long hours as a business manager, James thought his uncle's earnings went to sustain life in the fast lane, travelling around the country without any family to support. James had no inkling he would be the lucky beneficiary of his uncle's generosity.

James remembers thinking that the inheritance could not have arrived at a better time. His accounts were running on empty. Large credit card bills haunted him, but using plastic to pay plastic had become a habit. With his frantic efforts to make ends meet, James needed a break.

James's first thought when the letter came was "vacation!" Upon return from their two-week Caribbean cruise, Kim convinced him that they should redecorate the kitchen and living room. The couple then upgraded the furniture to match the upgraded lifestyle they planned with the new inheritance.

For three months James and Kim hit the best restaurants, went on weekend getaways, bought new clothes for everyone, and purchased a high-end home entertainment system. They had paid the outstanding balances on all their debts, including Kim's Honda Civic and their many credit cards. James arrived at our office with only $35,000 left in his savings account.

Although he had paid off his debt, it was too late for us to help James save the majority of his inheritance. Now the challenge would be to conserve what remained and to help him budget to avoid overextending himself again. One key problem: The habit of overextending credit cards is hard to break. For this reason, rushing out to pay all bills never makes sense. First, a new plan and new habits must be adopted.

At our suggestion, James agreed to use a portion of the remaining balance to set up an RESP for Randy and Ashton. We advised him to leave $5,000 in liquid savings and money-market accounts to meet any emergency cash requirements. The remaining $15,000 was spread among a mutual fund, municipal bonds, and T-bills to position James for growth of the remaining asset base.

We also worked through a budget with James to ensure that he and Kim would stick to a spending plan that fit their resources. The couple agreed to limit future travel to local road trips until James or Kim earned more. Restaurant bills were slashed in half. Kim went on a clothes budget, and James agreed to limit the upgrades of his multimedia entertainment system.

Had James properly managed his inheritance, he could have supplemented his family's income to make them more comfortable; provided for his children's education; and grown an asset base for his, Kim's, and his children's future.

Table 7-1 compares the growth of James and Kim's remaining $35,000 to the potential position had the couple chosen to preserve their capital. Assuming an investment at 8%, with all the earnings reinvested, after five years the $35,000 will have grown to $51,426 compared to the potential of $183,666 for the full inheritance. But after thirty years, the $35,000 would amount to only $352,193 compared to $1,257,832, a handsome sum that could have been grown from a modest inheritance. Now their challenge will be to hang on to what's left so they can increase it.

Table 7-1 Comparison of Investment Growth

	Amount Invested*	
Years Invested	Original Inheritance	Amount Remaining
0	$125,000	$35,000
5	183,666	51,426
10	396,521	111,025
30	1,257,832	352,193

At 8 percent annual return, all earnings reinvested.

Obviously, earning a steady 8% over 30 years requires intelligent investing as well as self-discipline. By leaving the principal untouched and reinvesting earnings, these returns can be produced with a balanced, medium-growth portfolio as illustrated with Michele Greene (Figure 7-3).

Instead, like too many unsophisticated new heirs, James attempted to create a new lifestyle instead of managing his inherited wealth.

GEORGE ALEXANDER: INHERITING MORE THAN MONEY

The son of a successful business owner, George Alexander faces transition at the helm of several family-owned-and-run businesses in the clothing industry. After growing up in the business, George's turn to accept control of the companies finally arrived. Although all his life he had prepared for that day, the full level of responsibility he faced for his family and his employees weighed on him. In addition to the memory of exceptional parents, George also encountered the expectations of future Alexander generations.

His personal life was also in transition. Just as he took over as chair of the board, George was preparing to marry. His own new family would have to be considered along with his reponsibilities to his sister and brother in any financial plan he made.

While George's financial situation is extraordinarily complex, the issues he faces provide lessons for us all. His inheritance involved not just one, but three, companies. Although similar in operation, each of the three entities had its own finances and records, and each entity was taxed separately. His parents had also set up a charitable foundation with its own assets, which he now had to oversee as chair of the board. Over the years, George also had amassed a significant amount of his own personal assets, as well as a growing RRSP account. To complicate matters even further, George had cross-collateralized, or shared, the risks among all of his personal and business interests (with the exception of the foundation). In other words, George readily transferred funds and assets between the many entities he managed. (To avoid tax problems, his accountant had made sure that proper paperwork reflecting these exchanges was prepared. For example, if one business needed cash, another would advance the cash as a corporate loan with written documentation.)

Despite his view of the wealth as a single basket to be managed and increased, George had not considered the overall allocation of his assets. He had cross-collateralized the risk, but not the asset allocation, of his wealth. Because of the complexity of George's financial situation, we set an immediate task of providing a simpler overview of his position. Like a map with too much detail, a complex re-creation of George's asset allocation would be difficult to navigate. By contrast, a summary of his combined personal and business assets would be much more helpful as a starting point for planning.

Even though his challenges were on a large scale, George shared with bookstore-owner Michele Greene a need for sufficient cash to cover potential business shortfalls. Each of George's businesses appeared to have sufficient working capital (funds for operations) to satisfy its own cash needs. But following his parents' lead, George operated from an extremely conservative stance in his estimations of liability and risk. This strategy protected the companies when the 1990s recession hit, but lower demand had sharply decreased growth in operations. The companies could survive the recession, but George felt stymied in his effort to increase assets to provide for his family and for the future. George came to us seeking growth through investment while his operations were in decline. Our review revealed an opportunity for long-term growth, lower risk, and higher returns through the permanent reallocation of his assets.

First, we determined the asset allocation for each individual entity. This step was only preparatory, the result was too complex to provide a useful overview. We then combined the allocations of each business to determine a combined asset allocation. We chose to exclude the assets of the foundation from this combined total since the legal restrictions placed on the management of the foundation and the use of its assets make the foundation a completely separate entity with a life of its own.

With this combined analysis in hand, George saw his cash-rich position. Understanding that almost 14% of his investments were in cash with an additional 14% in money-market accounts (see Table 7-4), he could now achieve returns superior to those offered by the separate money-market accounts in which each business left its working capital reserves. The combined allocation and the combined liabilities indicated that George could satisfy even the most conservative measures of liability with about 10% in cash, far less than the previous combined total of 28% in cash. This cash, as in the Michele case, could be moved to higher-yielding financial instruments, such as stocks, bonds, and commodities.

To ease George's concern for even the worst-case scenario (*i.e.*, a hurricane closing all three company sites simultaneously), he chose moderately liquid financial instruments, such as short-term deposits, bonds, equities, and foreign securities. Although an emergency conversion of some of these holdings to cash prior to the maturity date could be costly if it ever became necessary, the slight risk of such costs would be more than offset by the likelihood of higher returns in the interim.

Figure 7-4 George Alexander

Liquid Assets	Personal	RRSP	Business	Total	% Total
Cash	720,000	10,000	1,475,000	2,205,000	18.24%
Short-term Deposits	20,000	0	0	20,000	0.17%
Money Market }	90,000	450,000	1,010,000	1,550,000	12.82%
	0	20,000	40,000	60,000	0.50%
Federal Bonds	0	760,000	406,000	1,166,000	9.65%
Provincial					
Government Bonds	120,000	0	50,000	170,000	1.41%
Corporate Bonds	0	0	240,000	240,000	1.99%
Mutual Funds	250,000	0	0	250,000	2.07%
Stocks	0	16,000	0	16,000	0.13%
Foreign Securities	100,000	0	0	100,000	0.83%
Net Liquid Assets	1,300,000	1,256,000	3,221,000	5,777,000	47.80%
Non-Liquid Assets					
Ltd. Partnerships	50,000	50,000	0	100,000	0.89%
Personal Property	280,000	0	0	280,000	2.32%
Real Prop/Fixed Assets	1,570,000	0	1,900,000	3,470,000	28.71%
Notes Receivable	600,000	0	85,000	685,000	5.67%
Accounts Receivable	17,000	0	789,000	806,000	6.67%
Inventory	0	0	301,000	301,000	2.49%
Prepaids	0	0	127,000	127,000	1.05%
Cash Value Insurance	0	0	540,000	540,000	4.47%
Total Non-Liquid Assets	2,517,000	50,000	3,742,000	6,309,000	55.06%
Total Capitalization	$3,817,000	$1,306,000	$6,963,000	$12,086,000	100.00%
% Total	31.58%	10.81%	57.61%	100.00%	

In addition to underinvested cash, the analysis also revealed areas for reducing overhead. For example, transferring all of the accounts to one bank allowed for a significant reduction in banking fees, as well as enabling better overall management of the entities.

Although the assets were spread over several businesses, the combined asset allocation was inadequately diversified. Intuitively, George had thought that if his assets were spread among several different entities, his risk would be hedged by diversification. This belief, however, was only partially correct. Even though he held cash, bonds, and real estate in each of five different entities, he was still only holding cash, bonds, and real estate. George needed to diversify beyond these basic holdings.

While maintaining the independence of each of the entities, we used George's combined portfolio to determine the proper allocation of his assets. We sought to create a diversified total investment portfolio. To accomplish this, some of the cash from company A went into foreign securities and bonds; some of the cash from company B went into equities; and some of the cash from company C went into precious metals. Also, George bought a home for himself and his new wife from his personal funds, adding to the total amount of real estate.

In the end, George had diversified his family's entire estate and positioned it for long-term growth.

NEW HEIR'S CHALLENGES

Each of the families in this chapter faced challenges typically confronting new heirs. Although the size of Michele's inheritance vastly differed from that of Sarah's, both women were concerned about diversification. Sarah had an additional focus on taxes. In George's case, a simple overview was needed to allay his liquidity concerns and enable him to reinvest his cash for higher returns.

In each instance, a more sophisticated review of the situation enabled a more responsible use of the inheritance. While most apparent in the case of James Joseph, who had chosen to spend his inheritance on himself without seeking advice and without considering his options or the consequences, all the heirs improved their prospects by taking advice to responsibly manage their inheritances.

8

ADVICE ON ADVISORS

WELL-CHOSEN ADVISORS can help you think through each of your financial decisions connected with your inheritance, as well as advise you on estate issues. Whether your choice involves buying a home or deciding to place your RRSP in a self-directed plan, your investment decisions are supported by personal, expert advice. Most importantly, your advisors can provide, with your input, an overall financial strategy that fits together all the pieces of your financial picture. Rather than a haphazard, piecemeal approach, a professional team can work together, with your guidance, to integrate your financial issues into a coherent plan. Even if you have yet to inherit, choosing advisors now will give you time to establish a relationship before you are faced with bigger challenges, such as building an investment portfolio or dealing with the intricacies of estate planning.

Inheritors of smaller estates may first come into contact with advisors when receiving their inheritances, and this can be intimidating for the uninitiated. Even for those used to dealing with legal, accounting, and other professionals, the myriad of estate details at such an emotional time can seem overwhelming.

To use your advisors well, the first requisite is *trust*. Advisors must have your own best interests in mind, not the ideas of your deceased spouse, if you are a widow, or your deceased parents. No matter what your personal position, using advisors well is a part of personal financial empowerment, that is hard to achieve if you don't feel in control. Family advisors sometimes take a paternalistic approach, especially with the aged, but you need advisors who will take time to explain basics you don't understand without making you feel intimidated or humiliated. So it is important to establish whether you need to select new advisors or you can work with those who are familiar with the estate because of their involvement with the will, trust, or tax returns.

TWENTY WAYS TO CUT COSTS AND EFFECTIVELY USE YOUR PROFESSIONAL TEAM

Here are twenty tips on using professionals effectively and efficiently. Each of these concepts on how to manage your professional team is discussed later in this chapter.

1. Be willing to hire and pay for competent professionals.
2. Delegate and don't second-guess.
3. Allow advisors to delegate.
4. Focus on the big picture.
5. Be consistent.
6. Moderate perfectionism.
7. Recognize that complex questions often do not have bottom-line answers.
8. Listen to advice and then be decisive.
9. Don't push every rule to the limit.
10. Take care of the administrative work of running your finances yourself wherever practicable.
11. Recognize that life involves trade-offs and take responsibility for your choices.
12. Use advisors as gatekeepers to those seeking investments and charitable contributions.
13. Plan and work in weeks, months, and years rather than in minutes, hours, and days.
14. Follow through in a timely fashion.
15. Give a limited power of attorney for specific projects if you will be on vacation or hard to locate; *do not* give a general power of attorney.
16. Be aware of a professional's time constraints and plan ahead.
17. Only demand deadlines when necessary.
18. Keep good professionals.
19. Encourage open, informal communication.
20. Courtesy and tact are free; use them even when you're footing the bill.

SELECTING THE RIGHT TEAM

Your choice of team members will depend upon the complexity of your affairs. If you have been successfully handling your own finances and preparing your own tax returns the idea of adding both an accountant and a lawyer to your life may be unnecessarily expensive. By contrast, if you have inherited a large estate, you may require several lawyers, accountants, private bankers, money managers, and others. Even with a modest inheritance, you should concentrate on finding the most competent lawyer and accountant that you can. These two professionals represent the minimum advisory group a person with a middle income should have. Even if you only meet once or twice together when you first receive your inheritance, seeking their advice is critical to avoiding heavy future costs for a modest outlay now.

Regardless of your particular situation, the question remains: "What will these professionals do for you?" Below is a discussion of the various advisors you may encounter or hire and the services you should expect from each of them.

ADVISORS

Lawyers

Receiving an inheritance calls for two activities that should be discussed and handled with a lawyer:

• Reviewing the estate closing, including the will and/or the living trust and the terminal tax return, to ensure that your benefactor's wishes were carried out; and,

• Preparing your own will and/or living trust so that your new assets will be protected for your family and/or for your chosen charity.

Estate planning doesn't happen just once. You need a personal advisor to help you ensure that with each significant change in your life — marriage, birth or adoption of children, divorce, death of a spouse, receipt of an inheritance, or the move to another tax jurisdiction — your estate documents are revised to reflect that change.

If you already use a lawyer for general personal and business advice, find out if that lawyer is familiar with estate planning. If not, ask her or him to refer you to a colleague who is. Keep your original lawyer in the loop since that person will be familiar with future changes and can alert you to changes in your assets or family that affect the will or living trust you have prepared.

Selecting the right lawyer for your needs may not be easy. A lawyer is usually the most expensive member of the team. Both price and quality vary tremendously in this field. If you do not have a lawyer now, talk to friends that do. Gather names of lawyers who receive positive reviews.

You could also ask other professionals you know, such as your accountant, or check with the provincial bar for lists of lawyers by area of expertise.

Another issue that arises in selecting lawyers (and other professionals) is the choice between big firms and small firms. Depending upon the complexity of your affairs, a big firm may be best able to serve your needs. Big firms generally assure quality control, but that assurance has two costs. On the one hand, your work will be handled by several people, meaning a loss of intimacy with your advisors. And nuances may be lost as different lawyers deal with the same issue. On the other, big firms tend to charge higher prices, which reflect the higher overhead costs of larger firms.

By contrast, small offices are flexible and usually less expensive. However, there is less review built into the system, so if a lawyer (or other small-firm professional) makes a mistake, it may not get picked up and corrected.

PAYING PROFESSIONALS: FEE ARRANGEMENTS

All professionals are under time and money constraints, bound on the one hand by the necessity to complete tasks according to the strictures of the profession and on the other by the need to keep costs within reason. But keep in mind that professional fees are negotiable, and considering creative fee arrangements may enable you to work most comfortably with your advisors.

One of the best ways to keep costs under control without omitting necessary work that may not appear important to you (like a lawyer's habit of documenting each step or an accountant's tax projections) is to set monthly or quarterly dollar *target amounts* for fees. Ask the professional to alert you when fees may exceed these pre-authorized amounts.

Another approach is to place the professional on a *retainer basis*, which provides both parties the comfort of maintaining the relationship at a fairly constant fee level. For people with continuous business activities that require constant professional interaction, retainers may be the most cost-effective fee basis.

Also consider *value-based billing*. Many professionals today will expect to be paid according to the value of their work and their engagement letters will state that expectation. Professionals who bring special expertise to million-dollar deals expect to be compensated accordingly, not simply by the hour. The flip side is also true: Several hours spent on a matter that saves only a few hundred dollars should cost you less than the putative hourly bill.

Explore your professional's willingness to work on other than a straight-time basis. But keep in mind, if professionals make concessions to you and cut costs on small matters, be willing to pay the upside when deserved.

When shopping for a lawyer, select at least two or three lawyers to interview, either in person or by phone. Take note of their responsiveness. If you do not receive a prompt call-back, you may assume the office is too busy to accept new business. Make sure that you have a good feeling about the professional and her or his staff. If your personalities don't click, no matter how strong the reference, think twice. The advisor is there to serve *you*; you have to be the one who feels comfortable.

Different lawyers have different policies about initial free meetings and price quotations. Without seeing the nature of the matter you wish to have handled, it is difficult for a lawyer to predict, much less quote, an exact fee. Most lawyers prefer to talk to you by telephone or meet briefly in person to determine the scope of your situation, but you need to be aware of the lawyer's professional limitations. One constraint is time. Another is the problem of potential clients taking away just enough information from the initial interview to do themselves harm and then blaming the lawyer for their own mistakes. (Some lawyers have even been sued by potential clients whom they never even represented.) The more completely and succinctly you present yourself initially, the better the estimates of cost you will receive.

A lawyer's fees are negotiable. Often lawyers will give you a flat fee for a definite task, such as drawing a will. If the lawyer charges on a hourly basis, try to obtain a range of time and cost beforehand.

Once you have shopped, expect to be asked to pay a retainer in advance that ranges from one-half to all of the initial amount of the work you are requesting. You will be asked to sign an *engagement letter*, outlining the lawyer's responsibilities as well as your own. Some lawyers and accountants, especially in large firms, will even ask your permission to obtain a credit report.

To underscore, as with all professionals, the most critical question is: "Do you feel comfortable enough with this person to reveal your innermost fears and needs?" If you do, you have potentially found your personal lawyer. If not, keep on shopping. In either case, the new reality of life remains: Either you are a lawyer or you need one.

Accountants

If you don't have one already, find an accountant who is familiar with the complexities of estate planning or with any other tax issues that may arise in receipt of your inheritance. Usually a Chartered Accountant (CA) is preferable to a bookkeeper or other tax preparer who may not be capable of the complex work, but experience and personality should be primary criteria in your choice. Be sure that the individual is familiar with your estate planning concerns. Don't let certification *per se* be the decisive factor in your choice of advisor — many CAs specialize, and estate planning may be outside the particular professional's area of expertise. Make your decision on a combination of experience, recommendations, personal rapport and fees.

In making your selection, you'll have to choose an appropriate individual or small or large firm just as you needed to in selecting a lawyer. As you consider accountants, be sure they can answer relevant questions such as "What steps can I take to save taxes on income from my inherited assets?" or "Would I be better off incorporating my business?"

Once chosen, your accountant should be kept well-informed. As your assets grow, new opportunities to arrange your affairs in accordance with tax laws arise. You'll need a professional who keeps up with these changes and has sufficient working knowledge of your personal financial affairs to help you think proactively.

In the past, some accountants were trained more with an eye to looking back at past events rather than focusing on projecting ahead for tax planning. Today, more accountants provide the kind of proactive advice that keeps their clients ahead of the game.

Accountants usually request a meeting with their clients in the fall to do year-end tax planning. At this point in the tax year, time allows for the shifting of income and deductions in line with earnings and changes in tax laws.

One difference between lawyers and accountants is the level of confidentiality required by the profession. Despite the sense that the information you are giving is confidential — and a good professional will keep it so — there is no legal protection for CAs in the form of the accountant-client privilege. Quite the opposite. Be careful: If you have questions that you think need legal protection, ask them of a tax lawyer, not an accountant. Further, an accountant's work papers are reviewable by Revenue Canada and the accountant must turn them over; by contrast, a lawyer is legally and professionally bound by *attorney-client privilege* not to turn over privileged documents.

A word on accountant personalities: Yes, there is such a thing as typecasting. If there's ever been a straight-laced, conservative, HP-grinding, spreadsheet-number-crunching professional, an accountant's the one. Sometimes talking to these numerical whizzes makes one's head spin. But, at least one of the authors likes to think, that any stereotype is the work of fiction.

With these two professionals — the lawyer and the accountant — forming the core of your team, it's important to make sure that you have coordinated information and strategy. Once these members of your team are chosen, bring them together and hold either a conference call or planning meetings at least once to set your initial strategy.

Money Managers

The money manager's job involves making your money grow by taking a fee (not a commission) for providing investment advice and then actually investing the money. These professionals come in as many varieties as there are investment vehicles, because most money managers, in spite of their attempts to balance your portfolio, come with built-in biases in one investment direction or another. The key: Make sure their biases match your own.

Money managers generally exercise fiduciary control over the money they manage, meaning they obtain the right to engage in trades and transfers once you have placed your money with them. Commercial bank money management divisions keep the funds within their institutions, investing them directly from there. Smaller managers work with *custodian* institutions or banks with whom they have established ongoing business relationships; therefore, the manager doesn't literally keep your money but depending upon the type of contract you sign, can exercise limited or very broad powers over your funds.

Horror stories in the news warn of the possibility for abuse of this power. Once you click with the manager's style and investment leanings, check client references directly. Ensure that you only give as much power over your funds as feels comfortable to you. You may decide to start with limited trading powers and then gradually add more general powers once you feel secure about trusting your money manager.

The size of your investment portfolio will determine whether you should or could employ the help of a personal money manager. For moderate portfolios over $100,000, a money manager should be considered unless you are comfortable investing yourself and you have a solid investment track record. Major estates over $250,000 should be professionally managed, or at least, professionally advised. Recognize when shopping for advisors that some money managers limit their work to millionaire clients with huge investment portfolios.

Portfolios under $100,000 are usually too small for professionals to manage individually because the potential commissions do not sufficiently compensate for the manager's work. Smaller portfolios can best benefit from money managers by investing in professionally managed money-market and mutual funds.

Money managers' fee structures are based upon a percentage of the money "under management," as they say in the business. Fees usually run from 1% to 2% of the money managed, although like most fees, these too are negotiable. The more money you have under management, the lower the percentage fee. Most managers operate with a graduated fee structure: The first monies invested are charged the highest percentage and the percentage decreases proportionately as the funds increase. For example, the first $500,000 may command a fee of 2%; the next $500,000, 1.5%; the next million, 1%. If you place a large amount under management, such as two or three million dollars, you can negotiate a lower flat fee for the entire sum.

You will have to provide guidelines and goals for the manager. A manager probably cannot deliver both high income and rapid growth simultaneously. If your primary need is a steady stream of cash, the money will be invested differently than if your focus is on long-term growth.

Money managers are regulated by the various provincial securities commissions where they must be listed as "Registered Investment Advisors" and are theoretically subject to voluminous securities codes. In practice, oversight by these commissions is not always consistent. So, when entrusting your hard-earned and inherited resources, the watchword is: Buyer beware.

Stockbrokers

A stockbroker's job is to sell stock. Most stockbrokers are paid on commission — no sale, no commission. While the industry is surrounded by research and financial advice, whenever you take "free" information from a stockbroker, or any other commission-based consultant, you're paying a price. No matter how well-intentioned and honest the person, stockbrokers need to sell stocks to eat.

Does this mean you should avoid stockbrokers? No. Just be clear about their mission. Stockbrokers can be great resources, once you have understood their area of expertise and use it correctly. Stockbrokers should not be your financial strategists. Your stockbroker can be a good source of information about stocks *once you have decided independently of the broker what portion of your assets belong in stocks and what growth profile you need.*

Stockbrokers often offer other services that do not depend on commissions. At a full-service brokerage house, you can also obtain *cash management accounts* (with chequing and debit card features); pension plans and RRSPs; and purchases of mutual funds and other types of investments.

Whether it's preferable to use a full-service broker or a discount house will depend on your level of sophistication and your volume of trades. Discount houses charge commissions that are about half those of full-service brokers, and most houses have a minimum commission for trades, no matter what the size, from $25 to $75. The commission struc ture is based on the number of transactions, the number of shares involved, and the price of each share.

In general, commission structures are set by the houses at 1% to 2%. Big institutions like banks pay less than 1/2% to engage in *block trades*, or trading of large amounts of the same stock, usually over 10,000 shares. If you have a money manager who in turn uses a house to trade at a discount, negotiate having the manager's savings passed along to you.

Comparatively speaking, the largest fee associated with trading small amounts of stock may be the minimum fee, which alone can represent a disproportionate amount of a trade of $1,000 or less. *Churning*, or unnecessary trading to generate commissions, also represents a potential trap for small and large investors alike. Repeated transactions are made even when a longer-term "buy and hold" strategy would have been more appropriate.

The other problem that you may encounter with full-service and discount brokerage houses is stock exposure that is riskier than you wish. Stockbrokers are influenced by corporate marketing efforts and incentive commission structures to push certain stocks — so make your personal risk tolerance clear.

With stockbrokers, as with money managers, you'll need to determine how much trading leeway to authorize. When a stockbroker wishes you to consider a particular investment opportunity, it's wise to talk it over specifically rather than authorize the broker to trade your account within general guidelines. If you want to delegate trading authority, in general, granting this discretion to a money manager represents a wiser choice since the money manager's fee will be paid irrespective of trades made.

If you are a small trader you should consider a discount house, but recognize that the higher commissions charged by larger houses include access to a wealth of research data. Therefore, if you want to educate yourself about stocks and the market, the $50 to $75 minimum at larger houses may be worth the price of the ticket.

Financial Planners

During the past several years, the proliferation of investment opportunities, including life insurance, mutual funds, segregated funds and annuities, has led to a parallel growth in the number of professional financial planners. While previously unregulated to a large extent, financial planners today are now subject to a host of qualifying courses, examinations and memberships that have for the most part brought some control and quality to this burgeoning segment of financial professionals. Nowadays, Canadians will find that many provinces have adopted, or are in the process of adopting, educational standards and codes of ethics that individuals have to pass and endorse before being allowed to refer to themselves as qualified "financial planners."

The Financial Planners Standards Council of Canada has risen to become the national body to which all qualified financial planners should belong in order to carry on a legitimate financial planning practice in Canada. For the past several years, individuals who completed a three-year plan of study through the Canadian Institute of Financial Planning graduated with the title "Chartered Financial Planner." This programme was taken over by the Standards Council and the designation changed to "Certified Financial Planner" (C.F.P.).

Other professional designations are offered through the Life Underwriters Association of Canada (L.U.A.C.) and the Canadian Securities Institute. The "Chartered Financial Consultant" (Ch.F.C.) is peculiar to the life insurance industry and is usually conferred after completing a curriculum similar in scope to the C.F.P. programme. It is often undertaken after an individual has also completed the Chartered Life Underwriter (C.L.U.) programme, which focuses on the intricacies of life and disability insurance, and estate planning. The Canadian Securities Institute (CSI) offers intensive training in the securities industry through a parallel programme of study leading to the "Canadian Investment Manager" designation (C.I.M.). This designation is conferred only after students have completed their Canadian Securities Course (C.S.C.). Graduates of these programmes can refer to themselves as "financial advisors," a designation the Canadian securities industry has carved out for itself.

Professional financial planners can be a valuable resource for most Canadians. This is because, as generalists in personal finance, they can help you organize your financial situation in ways that are not normally addressed by accountants and lawyers who are, by definition, far more focused as to what they do. Duly qualified financial planners will help you gain a perspective as to where you are financially, help you prioritize your goals, organize your current and future financial resources, and assist you in designing and implementing a financial and investment plan that is right for you.

It's important to remember that other members of your team — your accountant and lawyer — deal with specific details of your financial situation and normally provide you with excellent perspectives particular to each discipline. Having a Certified Financial Planner on board completes your team. His or her job is to help interpret and clarify the suggestions of other team players to ensure that you have a good idea of the overall thrust of your financial plan. If your financial planner is licensed to do so, he or she can actually implement many of the investments and strategies that are right for your particular situation. Accountants and lawyers are normally not licensed to deal with most types of investments. As a result, your financial planner should be a graduate of the Certified Financial Planner programme, the Canadian Securities Course and the Canadian Investment Manager programme. If your financial planner is also licensed through a provincial insurance commission too, then all the better for you.

When looking for your financial planner, though, be aware of the costs involved, just as you would when choosing your accountant and lawyer. Today, qualified financial planners are either commissioned, fee-only, or a combination of both. Whichever method you choose is ultimately up to you. Dealing with a commissioned-based financial planner will always incur a certain amount of risk. This is because "commissions" is still a dirty word in Canada, perhaps as a carry-over from the old days when slick-talking "salesmen" sold you a car, insurance policy or vacuum cleaner you didn't need or want. Today, commissioned-based financial planners are paid on the basis of the financial products you choose to help complete your financial plan.

Fee-only planners do not charge commissions; they are hired on an hourly basis and you will pay anywhere from $100 per hour and up for their advice. A financial planner hybrid is someone who charges you an hourly rate — often less than the usual rate — but who also receives a commission based on the products you deem appropriate to your needs. Fee-only based financial plans can cost anywhere from $750 and up, often exceeding $5,000 for sophisticated financial plans. Commission-based financial planners can earn equal amounts for their services, except that their income is often buried in the financial products you choose.

When you consider the costs incurred by using accountants and lawyers ($200 per hour), hiring a fee-only financial planner only adds to the costs of your team. Remember, too, that fee-only planners, like lawyers and accountants, often have an additional cost in the form of an annual retainer, and, unless licensed, will not be able to offer advice about the financial products you should purchase. The difficulty with commission-based financial planners is that they may have a vested interest in recommending one financial product over another because of higher commissions paid. There is no way you can insulate yourself completely from this kind of activity. However, you *should avoid* dealing with financial planners who represent just one financial company that pushes its own financial products, regardless of how wide their product selection. In today's confusing world of financial products and services, always *look for an independent financial planner who has no particular axe to grind and can offer just about any product available in the financial market place*.

General Insurance Agents

Your insurance agent should help you tie all of your insurance together, making sure, for example, that your homeowner's policy contains a general liability *umbrella* clause to protect you in case of lawsuits that arise from accidents on your property.

A good agent with whom you have developed a long-standing relationship can be worth his or her weight in gold. If you buy a new car, he can issue a binder by phone. If you live in an area prone to natural disasters he can make sure you are adequately covered.

Just remember, the agent's fees come from sales, so check with your team before adding substantial or expensive products to your portfolio.

Real Estate Agents

While some people don't think of a real estate agent as part of the financial team, a long-term relationship with the same agent can keep you in good stead, whether you're buying or selling a property. When selling, even in a city some miles distant from the agent, you can always have your agent place the sale with a local agent. Your agent will earn some part of the fee and will look after your best interests.

If buying, likewise, use the agent to negotiate for you independently of the selling agent. (Technically, both agents are paid by the seller from the commission on the sale of the house.) Your agent should be familiar with your needs and know how far you would want to take a negotiation. Even if you are a lawyer (and if you're not, a lawyer should always check all real estate documents), like any other buyer you are better off negotiating at arm's length. Having an agent gives you time to think while in the midst of a rapid exchange of offers and counter-offers, whereas if you are on the front line negotiating for yourself, you might get blown away. If you don't know an agent or broker you can trust, use your lawyer to represent you.

Using Family Advisors or Selecting Your Own: Your Choice

When dealing with large estates, family ties often include a set of advisors to be inherited along with the money. Lawyers, accountants, trust officers, and money managers have psychological investments in past decisions, which may not fit your needs.

If your inheritance comes with professionals attached, remember that their loyalties may lie elsewhere, with other family members or even with the past. To gain a sense of whether these advisors can serve your needs, meet with each one separately and elicit his or her point of view about topics that matter to you. Establish whether you feel comfortable around each individual. You will want the feeling that you could call at four in the morning and that advisor would stand ready to help.

If you are comfortable with the existing advisors, establish your own priorities by communicating with them clearly. Ask the advisor to confirm your understanding of his or her role and professional fees with a new engagement letter, even if the professional has served the family over a long period of time.

If you don't feel comfortable, you'll need to shop for other advisors. Once you make up your mind to change, avoid too much explanation so as to avoid alienating your family and former advisors. You do not need to overexplain — you have an absolute right to choose the professionals you wish.

MANAGING YOUR TEAM

Inheritances come in many sizes, from a $25,000 parents' savings account to a multimillion-dollar fortune grown several generations back. Team sizes need to match inheritance sizes. For more modest inheritances, a small team, composed primarily of a lawyer and/or an accountant, will do.

For larger inheritances, a more sophisticated approach is desirable. You will want to build a solid professional team, which may include many of the different types of advisors described above, to maximize the growth and use of your inheritance.

THE 4M FORMULA FOR ADVISORS BOX

ॐ
Modest:
One meeting with a lawyer or an accountant is necessary to put your inheritance in order, assuming that the executor is competent. A financial planner can assist you in organizing your financial situation and help you keep it on track.

ॐ
Moderate:
At least one meeting with both a lawyer and an accountant plus some time with someone, such as an appropriately qualified financial planner, regarding your investment direction should do the trick.

ॐ
Major:
You will want to build a professional team to include, at minimum, a lawyer and an accountant. You should also consider adding other professionals discussed, such as a Certified Financial Planner to your team. Plan to meet once a year to ensure a fit for your inheritance into your existing income, tax, and investment picture and to continue implementation. You also need professional advice to revise your estate plan. Estate planning is a must.

ॐ
Millions:
You should build a professional team that you can grow with as you preserve and increase your inheritance. Work with your advisors to coordinate an overall estate, tax, and investment plan.

Whether you have just one lawyer or several advisors, you are the leader of a team that includes you as a member. Some argue that great leaders are born, others that great leaders are made. In either case, using proven management techniques will help you to enhance the performance of your personal professional team.

Effective delegation and supervision, accomplished by communication, stand at the core of a good management style. Through *supervision, communication,* and *information,* you can efficiently manage and coordinate the efforts of your team in the most efficient manner. Assign tasks in accordance with the individual abilities of team members since certain tasks, such as tax planning, could be undertaken by more than one team member. Also recognize that some tasks, such as overall planning, should be handled by team members collectively. Assign tasks using general objectives mutually established by you and your advisors. For example, "By September 15, I would like to have a new strategy for my growth-oriented investments. Be sure to explain my options and any legal or tax implications as well."

Communication can be achieved through both formal and informal means. Facilitate communication among your advisors by copying them on key documents, calling regularly, and meeting occasionally. You will be able to supervise their activities, assign tasks efficiently, and increase the flow of information.

The point of having these legal and financial advisors is to gain information for effective decision making. Up-to-date news also allows you to shift tactics to meet legislative changes, economic movements, or to respond to crises.

ACT AS A LEADER

Most great leaders exhibit the ability to inspire through personality or example. Earning respect often requires more than charisma. Sensitivity to the needs and strengths of individuals on the team can inspire the right kind of loyalty and productivity. While many captains are aware of the needs of the team as a whole, powerful leaders can recognize the individuality of each member of the team.

Exhibiting your own dedication clearly inspires others. When you are committed to doing something and you are willing to sacrifice yourself to achieve the goals you have set, people respond in kind. In the corporate world, a company president who has shown that he or she is willing and able to take any job in a manufacturing plant gains an enormous response in employee productivity. (The Japanese actually require most of their executives to be able to do any job in the company.) For a new heir, showing the willingness to understand technical financial matters provides this kind of leadership.

Don't confuse respect with *positional power*. As an heir, especially to substantial wealth, you may experience immediate deference, but you'll have to earn respect.

The most effective form of authority is *personal power*, which is derived from working *with*, not simply directing, team members. People with personal power are able to have others respond to their wishes because *they* asked and not because "they're the boss and they said so."

This simple policy common to many strong leaders should be followed: acknowledge the strengths and interests of the individuals you meet — and encourage them to fulfill their own potential. For example, if your accountant also has an investment bent, allow that person to share ideas for portfolio growth. If your lawyer's lifework includes an interest in international investments, welcome the information she or he can bring to the table. In both individual and group settings, affirm strengths. When team members sense this consideration coming from you, they respond in kind.

MAINTAIN LONG-TERM PROFESSIONAL RELATIONSHIPS

In the development of a long-term relationship with your advisors you will establish mutual trust and improve the level and quality of service you receive. You'll better understand the abilities of your advisors, which will improve your ability to assign responsibilities, and they will better understand your wants and needs, which will improve their ability to service you.

Most professionals will go the extra mile for clients they really care about. In the busy world of professional life, no amount of money can command loyalty for a client who is perceived as difficult to serve or who constantly changes advisors. So once you are comfortable with your advisors, stick with the people who have invested time and energy in getting to know you, not just your affairs as they appear on paper. Long-term relationships will save you money too, so like a new couple, new professionals (and clients) must be courted.

HOLD REGULAR PLANNING MEETINGS

Whether you have a modest inheritance and meet only once with your sole advisor or you inherit a large estate and hold quarterly meetings with your professional team, any budget for professional services, large or small, should include periodic planning meetings, even if only once every two or three years. Aside from the initial meeting, when your team will obtain a complete overview of your situation, these meetings enable you to develop your relationship, allow open communication, and enable brainstorming with the team. Even if your inheritance is very small and may not warrant this kind of attention, if at all feasible, use such periodic meetings to help enrich your regular income and investment activities.

One heir complained about the cost of meetings, feeling they were a "waste of time" and nothing was accomplished. She cancelled all advisory meetings for a year. At the end of the year, her professional costs had risen because none of the professionals were conversant with what the others were doing and no one was responsible for reinvesting her dividends. At the end of the year, 25% of her assets were in cash. The lack of coordination had cost her several hundred thousand dollars in lost income, all for want of a $1,000 meeting! While this example may seem extreme, it happens on a smaller scale whenever a team doesn't have a chance to work together.

In order to run a meeting effectively, create an agenda and save new business for the end of the meeting. Don't follow the example of one heir, who came late to each meeting, while his advisors waited in a conference room, their "fee-clocks" ticking, the client would often spend the next fifteen minutes making telephone calls about lunch appointments and basketball tickets.

Instead, come prepared. Read all the materials your professionals have prepared for you in advance and write down specific questions. Allow some time for dialogue on each issue — don't always demand a bottom line, because often no bottom line exists. Rather, a series of decision-trees branch out in several directions, and choices made to reach one or more viable alternatives, each with different ramifications. For example, if you ask, "What's the bottom line, should I invest in this property or not?", at best you'll get only a partial answer. If you ask instead, "How does this investment affect my asset allocation? How does it affect my growth? How does it affect my taxes?", you'll elicit a perspective that will aid you in making the decision. Also remember to ask: "What would be a better choice?"

HOW TO COMPLAIN AND GET
THE RESULTS YOU WANT

In the world of commercial transactions, things will sometimes go wrong for the consumer. If you find yourself in the position of having to complain about services, tried and true techniques will increase the likelihood of your getting results. Here are seven pointers for systematically achieving the best results.

1. *As a preventive measure, establish yourself as a preferred customer.*
    By becoming a regular and familiar client, you will receive good service in the first place. This practice will usually save you from having a reason to complain.

2. *Before you complain, outline the problem for yourself and clarify how you would like it resolved.*
    Put down on paper exactly what you perceive is wrong, as best as you can, including when the "symptoms" began, what they are, and what the "diagnosis" is. Once you can state the problem and preferred solution precisely, you are closer to resolution. Simply griping without specifics can sour any situation.

3. *Be organized: as a routine habit, keep copies of all correspondence and bills.*
    If you have a legitimate concern about a professional bill, check your own notes of each conversation with that professional. Check to see what it is you have authorized the professional to do, how much time was spent talking about it on the phone, and what your price expectations were based upon.

    If the complaint is about the quality of the service rendered, your own correspondence with the professional will assist you in deciding how to tackle the problem. In addition, review your file and notes about the problem at hand and see what obvious issues arise in your own review. Trust your ability to engage in such a review.

4. *Decide on the best person to complain to and the best means of reaching that person, whether by letter, telephone, or personal visit.*
    In most cases, you should first bring up the problem, whatever it is, directly with the professional and try to resolve it. But in some instances, another approach will be necessary. If you are dealing with a lawyer or an accountant in a large firm, then you may request to speak with someone higher up the corporate ladder if your concern is not resolved.

5. *If you can't get a satisfactory resolution dealing directly with the firm in question, it's time to turn to a professional or government organization.*

If approaches within the establishment do not work, remember that every professional, whether fee or commission-based, is governed by some statutory authority. For lawyers, it is the provincial bar; for accountants, the Canadian Institute of Chartered Accountants' provincial affiliate; and for money managers and commission-based professionals, the provincial securities commissions. In addition, if you feel the matter extends beyond professional performance and into the problems of malfeasance or fraud, seek competent legal advice.

In general, when dealing with professionals or with any other situation requiring complaint satisfaction, if in doubt, start at the top. Whether you have a problem involving a large amount of money, a policy variation, or a waiver, avoid getting a "no" lower down the authority ladder. Once people have dug themselves into a corner it's harder for those higher up to intervene, whereas one of the prime functions of bosses is to decide when to make exceptions to the rulebook.

6. *Keep your cool at all costs.*

Remember that angry accusations will very likely elicit an angry or defensive response and give the person with whom you are dealing the excuse to decide that the real problem is your personality rather than a legitimate complaint. In legal circles, the professional complainer is known as a "litigious" person, and being tagged with this label is the "kiss of death."

Start out with a strong, clear statement of your case: "This is what happened, and this is what I want done." Don't be tentative as in, "This is what happened ... I think ... but I don't know if you can do anything." You are risking, not engaging, the full attention and action from the individual you are approaching.

Whatever you do, don't begin with the threat of legal action. Court is the appeal of last resort, not the first option in a complaint process.

7. *Figure out the "opportunity cost" of making and resolving your complaint before you pursue it to the fullest extent.*

Spending $300 to solve a $100 complaint doesn't make economic sense, and you may destroy a valuable professional relationship in the process. Unless "being in the right" is really worth the psychic and economic hassle, you may prefer to temper your complaint with considered action. Remember that powerful people choose their battlegrounds carefully.

SPECIAL PROBLEMS WHEN YOU
CAN'T FIRE TEAM MEMBERS

There are two times when you may have no choice over the professionals on your team: during the estate settlement stage when you are working with an executor chosen by your benefactor and also throughout the life of a trust if you are the beneficiary.

Your relationship with the executor, unless a family member, can normally end within a year at the windup of the estate unless the estate is terribly complex or the will is subject to court challenge.

With trustees, however, your challenge may be to get along for years with people whose ideas and objectives seem diametrically opposed to your own. With these folks, as in any situation that involves give and take, good negotiating techniques are a must. While a full-scale negotiation course is beyond the scope here, some key negotiating techniques are:

- Try to see the other side's point of view.
- Work from a non-confrontational stance, using facts and logic, rather than emotion, to make your points.
- Empathize with the other side's entire position, not just their stated goals, including the personal and institutional imperatives that drive the people with whom you are negotiating.
- Be persistent. If you reach a stalemate return again at a future date.

Keep in mind that even if you do not favour a professional with whom you must work, the relationship will continue, at least for a limited duration. That means, where possible, treat these individuals with the same courtesy you do the other advisors on your team, and maintain a professional relationship at all times to ensure that you do not jeopardize your rights and privileges because of a personality conflict.

KEEPING PROFESSIONAL COSTS
UNDER CONTROL

People of substance tend to use professionals more than the average person, and indeed they often need more advice as their finances tend to be more complex. The following tips (summarized from above) will help you to use your advisors in the most cost-effective manner. Some of these tips might seem obvious, but you would be surprised to find how often otherwise smart people fail to heed them.

1. *Hire and be willing to pay for competent professionals.* You have to work with, rely upon, and assign matters to people you can trust. Good professional advice is expensive. Bad professional advice is even more expensive.

2. *Assign and don't second-guess.* When you assign matters to your professional advisors, outline your goals and then allow time for results to be achieved. Don't try to oversee *how* they are achieved. The habit of second-guessing is costly, especially when it creates an atmosphere of fear or animosity among those who work for you.

3. *Allow advisors to delegate.* Be aware that you can save money if professionals are able to delegate work efficiently among themselves. Also, for matters that don't require the professional's direct attention, use the professional's assistant.

4. *Focus on the big picture.* Let others focus on the details and let them get on with their tasks unless they ask for your help.

5. *Be consistent.* Don't give mixed signals about your intentions regarding responsibilities. If you want to personally manage more and delegate less, do so keeping your advisors in the picture.

6. *Moderate perfectionism.* Being a perfectionist costs money. If you are willing to put up with only moderate standards of performance, less expensive personnel can do more tasks for you. Also, perfectionism causes professionals to overprepare, which can be costly. Don't nitpick!

7. *Recognize that complex questions often do not have bottom-line answers.* Don't shortcut the process of discovery and discussion, or you may lose valuable knowledge that should be learned now, not later.

8. *Listen to advice and then be decisive.* Once your team has offered its expert opinions, extending decisions and continuing to explore options is more costly and usually does not necessarily produce better results. This also means avoiding "cocktail-party wisdom." Every advisor has clients who go to parties, meet other professionals, pick their brains, and come back with instant solutions.

9. *Don't push every rule to the limit.* Many rules have exceptions and there are endless grey areas in the law. Clients who attempt to push the limits of every rule, much like tired children pushing their parents, stress their advisors and run up unnecessarily high bills.

10. *As much as possible, take care of the administrative work of running your finances, yourself.* Do your own meeting scheduling, coordinate your own conference calls, and draft your own letters. Do your own footwork, getting the basic information, rather than

paying professionals for information that you can get yourself. Keep track of documents. Every time you ask for duplicates, it costs the professional (and you) staff time.

11. *Recognize that life involves trade-offs and take responsibility for your own choices.* If your income is high, you may choose to pay others to fight life's financial, legal, and paperwork battles for you, freeing yourself to enjoy the money you have. If you choose to let others do the work for you and it costs money, even a lot of money, look at the costs of the alternatives. If money was saved or made because others kept track; or if your time was well spent in enjoyable activities while your professional advisors "minded the store"; don't begrudge the money you spent. Remember that time is money and even if a significant portion of your income goes to others for services, it may be still worthwhile if it allows you time to pursue your own interests.

12. *Use advisors as gatekeepers to those seeking investments and charitable contributions.* Remember that advisors can act as gatekeepers for you. Good advisors can screen out requests for investments and contributions, helping you select the best opportunities. Recognize that gatekeeping also brings power. Many gatekeepers gain in power as a result of helping you select ventures and charities to support. Remember, to many middle-income professional gatekeepers, having the opportunity to influence the course of events, even secondhand, is the privilege of the advisory position. If you enjoy the day-to-day power brokering, by all means require that all requests be routed to you directly and then use the advisor to render an opinion for you. Or, do as some donors do, and delegate the "no's," saving the "yes's" for yourself. From your point of view, the salient questions are: "Do I need or want the extra hassle and exposure of dealing with all the requests?"; and, "Am I willing to pay the price of screening?"

13. *Plan and work in weeks, months, and years rather than minutes, hours, and days.* The more planning you can build into your activities, the easier it is for professionals to service you cost-effectively.

14. *Follow through in a timely fashion.* Repeated attempts to finish the same project are costly. Information and momentum are lost. It costs time and therefore money for professionals to refresh themselves about an old project each time the subject is brought back.

15. *Give a limited power of attorney for specific projects if you will be on vacation or hard to locate; do not give a general power of attorney.* While a general power of attorney is unnecessary and inadvisable unless you will be on an extended trip (and even then you'd want to know the professional well since she or he could, in theory, take control), a limited power of attorney can allow your professional to move ahead on deadlines within the parameters you have established.

16. *Be aware of a professional's time constraints and plan ahead.* Most professionals are busy (and you don't want a professional who isn't busy, do you?) so you need to dove-tail their schedules, with yours where possible. You should also try not to intrude on professionals' holidays. Professionals lead busy lives with many demands from their clients, colleagues, and communities. They need their holidays and vacations for recreation. Lonely people with money often decide to engage in transactions during the holiday season — and guess who they call? Unless you are dealing with an actual emergency, save it for January 2.

17. *Only demand deadlines when necessary.* Demanding immediate attention often requires professionals to inefficiently rearrange their schedules which, if done unnecessarily or repeatedly, may both strain the relationship and cause the professional to treat such demands as "crying wolf." Also, many clients will make time demands on their advisors but will not reciprocate in kind. Because some clients constantly violate this rule, the obvious should be reinforced: Do not demand a report tomorrow if you are not going to read it for a month.

18. *Keep good professionals.* Once you've made informed decisions and picked your team, create an atmosphere of trust. Set up mutually agreed-upon review times for updating your plans, and stick with the professionals you have chosen.

19. *Encourage open, informal communication.* In a more relaxed setting, professionals may share ideas that they may hold back in more formal office settings.

20. *Courtesy and tact are free; use them even when you're footing the bill.* Surprisingly many otherwise astute people have missed the point that treating others with consideration produces better results. Often people will go out of their way for you (and it won't cost extra) if you go out of your way to acknowledge their contributions.

If you follow these tips, you will save money because your professionals will produce more effective work. But remember, if your goal is to free up your time to enjoy your inheritance, you will have to pay for the privilege. Strike the right balance between doing things for yourself and having them done within budget by others.

Don't assume that merely because you are paying the money, you will get the kind of advisory input you think you need. Being rich, or even a paying customer, doesn't make you right. Assume that the professional's time is as important as yours, give respect to what professionals say (otherwise, why did you hire them?) and recognize that your team only functions as effectively as its leader.

PART THREE

PROVIDING
FOR THE FUTURE

9

𝕩

PLANNING YOUR ESTATE

AMONG CIVILIZED HUMANS, no two topics are more feared or inevitable than death and taxes. Estate planning combines both. Whether you are a new or expectant heir, the child who will inherit from parents, the parent who will be leaving an estate, or the beneficiary of a trust, you need to conquer the basics of estate planning. Because estate planning involves dealing with your own death or that of a family member or friend, it is a sensitive chore approached with seriousness and difficulty.

The laws of inheritance regulate the disposition of private property after the owner's death. The will or trust sets out your property plans. If you do not prepare a will or trust, provincial intestacy laws will designate your heirs for you.

Dying intestate, or without a will or trust, can cause major problems for your relatives. The process of closing your estate becomes burdensome and the province's choice of heirs might not match your own. Failing to take care of your loved ones by not planning for their future is the ultimate discourtesy.

SIX GOOD REASONS TO PLAN YOUR ESTATE

Even though the prospect of death may seem remote, there are good reasons to create a will and where appropriate trusts:

1. To ensure that your spouse will inherit as much of your separate estate as you wish and also meet her spousal legal entitlements;
2. To specify who should take care of minor children if both parents die simultaneously;
3. To choose an administrator for the estate;
4. To make specific bequests to charities, friends, or relatives in your will;
5. To ensure as far as possible the predictability of tax consequences; and
6. To ensure liquidity and funding to pay taxes.

PLANNING THE FUTURE WITH TOOLS OF THE PAST

Like voting, the right to make disposition of your property developed over time from the ambit of the privileged few to the right of the many. Nonetheless, the past still influences estate planning making the process virtually unintelligible to the average person.

For example, provincial legislation requires that if dependent children are omitted from a will, the Court may appoint the Provincial Guardian to protect their right to adequate financial provision from the estate. While forgetting one's children may sound far-fetched today, in an earlier time, the recognition of legitimate and illegitimate heirs was a topic of great significance. For, as the story goes:

> A rich dying man called his lawyer to him for the purpose of disposing of his worldly goods. "How many children have you?" the lawyer asked.
>
> "That, sir," said the old-timer, "will be decided by the courts when my will is contested."

As you approach the subject of estate planning, whether as the beneficiary or the benefactor, keep in mind that its complexities derive from two contrapuntal themes: the burden of the historical past and the necessity to project into the future every possible or foreseeable outcome.

The contemplation of possible future outcomes and the provision for every contingency in the language of the will in the context of the overall estate plan is a topic that does not come easily to most people. The play, *Daddy's Dying, Who's Got the Will?* successfully captures the preoccupation with inheritance and the concept of stewardship of the land in farming communities. By contrast, the average city dweller thinks of inheritance only in terms of a single generation. Yet when preparing a will, you need to anticipate all possible scenarios for the future as for instance where one or more of your potential heirs dies before their parents, requiring contingent planning of your estate.

Signing a modern will derives from medieval rights to property. In the Middle Ages, in order to convey property from one person to another, a clod of earth from the property was literally handed from one man to another. This rite, called *seisin*, required several witnesses to observe and validate the ceremony since it was conducted without the benefit of paper. Likewise, the signing of a completed will today, although considerably more relaxed, harkens back to this earlier time. Most provinces require formal will-signing ceremonies. In general, one or more disinterested persons must witness the signing in order for the will to be valid.

Unlike many contracts concluded without the benefit of a lawyer, few people prepare their own wills because of the complexity of this area of the law. Since such a large number of requirements derive from our Western historical past, technical expertise is mandatory.

YOUR ESTATE

Much of estate planning is the flip side of closing the estate of the deceased. You'll need to make choices about living wills, burial, and the beneficiaries of your will or trust. If you have minor children, you'll need to select guardians. The primary issue that you'll face as donor, however, wasn't even considered in your role as recipient of the estate — taxes arising on death.

Most estate planning involves tax issues, especially with larger estates. Under current tax law, the estate of the deceased will pay tax of approximately 40% on capital gains deemed to be triggered on death on appreciated capital property of the deceased.

Although most heirs of substantial estates make a formal estate plan, 60% of all estates transfer through the intestacy laws. So before we discuss formal estate planning, let's see what happens if you die without a valid will or living trust.

WHAT HAPPENS IF YOU DIE INTESTATE?

If you fail to make an estate plan for yourself, the court will make one for you that includes disbursing the property, picking a guardian for your children, and selecting an administrator. Without a will, you will also not be able to leave a gift to your university or favourite charity since intestacy laws do not provide for charitable gifts.

Whether you fail to make a will, or have an old one and don't update it, the State will step in. Each province's *property and intestacy laws determine who will receive what portion of your estate.* You must check your own province's laws to determine how the intestacy laws would specifically apply to you.

In general, spouses receive one-third to one-half of the estate and *issue*, i.e., each of your children (who may or may not include adopted children), receive their allocation of the estate assets.

If you do prepare a will but subsequently remarry, and the current spouse is omitted, she will get her intestate share under the relevant provisions of provincial LPA.

Likewise, the province's Official Guardian will step in to remedy the failure to mention a specific child in a will to ensure that the omitted child gets his or her share of the estate.

THE 4M FORMULA FOR ESTATE PLANNING

❧

Modest:
Have a lawyer prepare a will or living trust to distribute your estate. If you have minor children, be sure to appoint legal guardians.

❧

Moderate:
Retain a lawyer to draft a trust document and will to distribute your estate. Also consider the appropriate use of will substitutes such as life insurance and jointly-held property. These assets automatically pass to the survivor or beneficiary upon death. Make sure the beneficiaries are properly designated.

❧

Major:
Consult with your lawyer and prepare an irrevocable or testamentary trust to minimize your tax liability on death. If you are married, make sure to make use of the tax-free transfer of assets to a spouse and always obtain his/her formal written concurrence to transfers of assets to others.

❧

Millions:
Work with an estate-planning specialist to develop a long-term strategy to minimize your tax liability on death and implement your estate. You may also wish to consider the income and tax benefits of using charitable trusts.

PLANNING WITH PROFESSIONALS

As a new heir, estate planning should be part of your financial arsenal. Be well informed so that you make effective use of your estate-planning professionals.

While you may properly engage in a certain amount of self-help, preparing your own will from kits or even computer programs should be approached with caution. Even the simplest estate and family structure will require both a lawyer and an accountant. Don't have just anyone calling themselves a "financial planner" put together your estate. And be forewarned, if you plan a large estate without competent advice, the likelihood is that your mistakes may cost your heirs more in legal fees and taxes later than you may save now by doing it all yourself.

An estate-planning lawyer tells the story of a client who didn't trust lawyers. Instead, he chose to use a will kit he bought from a stationery store. When filling in the blanks on the pre-printed will form he wrote, "I give all my *personal* property to my wife." He did not make any residuary bequests or bequests covering anything else he did not specifically gift away. As a result, when he died the house he owned (by far his largest asset), fell into intestacy. He had only devised his personal property, not his real property. Under the intestacy laws, his children were entitled to half of the house and only reluctantly agreed, after a legal battle, to let their stepmother stay in her home.

In this case, because the client did not know the legal distinction between real and personal property, his estate plan was completely undermined. Self-help in this case was much more costly than the legal fees for a properly prepared will.

ESTATES AND TAXES

Decisive factors to be considered in your estate planning will be: (a) spousal rollovers, (b) rollover of "Qualified Farm Property" to children and grandchildren, and (c) the utilization of the Capital Gains Deduction for: "Qualified Farm Property" and "Shares of a Small Business Corporation" (SBC).

PLANNING CONSIDERATIONS

The motivation behind your estate plan will be to provide for the orderly devolution of your wealth at minimum tax cost and thus will likely incorporate the following necessary key elements:

• provide liquidity on death to meet immediate claims against your estate including taxes and probate;

• provide for durable powers of attorney for property and for personal care; and

- provide for certainty and predictability of tax consequences by will and by programmed giving during your lifetime.

A TRUST, A WILL, OR BOTH?

The choice of document or documents to prepare your estate plan is dependent primarily on two factors: your current individual circumstances and your anticipated estate position on death. To make the choice you will have to consider your objectives, the size and composition of your estate, your marital status, your age, and the type of holdings in your estate. These non-tax factors should always be your first priority.

Whether you choose a *formal witnessed will*, a *holographic will* (from the Greek "wholly written," meaning a handwritten will, which is allowed in some jurisdictions), a living will or revocable trust, an irrevocable trust, or a combination of one or more of these instruments, depends on the complex interplay between individual objectives, and tax law and probate costs.

Remember that trusts themselves are divided into a number of types, each with a specific objective and tax treatment. Trusts have the practical effect of controlling the uses to which the trust funds can be put after the trust is executed, therefore, trusts are almost as complex and varied as human relationships themselves because they're the legal expressions of the settlor's desires and fears.

Testamentary trusts, created by will at the death of the settlor, cannot be modified except by the express modification provisions, if any, contained in the will. *Inter vivos* trusts, set up to take effect during the life of the trust settlor, include both revocable living trusts and irrevocable trusts (see Chapter 4, Trust Terms, pages 39–41). Revocable living trusts can be modified or cancelled so long as the grantor is alive. Once created, irrevocable trusts cannot be changed without going to court, except within the parameters established in the original trust document.

While there's not a strict one-to-one correlation between trust type and tax rule, each major trust type has a specific tax treatment under the *Income Tax Act*. For example, living wills and revocable trusts, used to avoid probate for ease of administration and for flexibility do not avoid the tax consequences of the death of the settlor.

If your estate only bears moderate capital gains exposure and your concern is mainly to have your estate pass hassle free to your immediate family, you may employ a trust *inter vivos* in combination with a will. The will would cover residual gifts (for property left outside the trust) and guardianship appointments.

Then there are the wealthy, who pay taxes on death on their appreciated estate assets at a rate of 40%. To minimize the impact of these taxes, a variety of tax planning tactics are required. Further estate plans will usually be specifically designed to meet other objectives, such as preserving wealth for several family generations and making significant donations to charity. The bigger the estate, the more complex the estate plan is likely to be, prompted in part by tax avoidance and in part by the desire to leave a mark on the world. In the next chapter, we will discuss ways to minimize your estate's potential tax liability.

SMALL ESTATES

For small estates, tax planning depends upon the type of assets and, to some extent, your age. A young person wouldn't ordinarily set up a revocable living trust when a simple, less expensive will suffices. A will avoids the hassles involved in transferring title each time assets turn over as the young adult progresses through life. However, if the same young person has only a mother to support and he owns a condominium, a revocable living trust would allow his home to pass directly to her without probate cost or delay.

On the other hand, a young businesswoman with a business partner would have to think twice about a revocable living trust because placing the business assets in the trust could involve additional paperwork for every transaction, possibly inhibiting both business dealings and credit opportunities. For her too, a will would work best.

For couples, your main concern will be providing for your spouse to inherit hassle free and also for your children if they are minors. You may wish to consider setting up a testamentary spousal trust, but make sure that as your estate grows with your investments, you adjust your will and estate plan as necessary.

The type of your holdings may also affect your estate plan. If you have no heirs and live with your long-time same-sex companion, estate planning may involve putting your entire holdings in joint tenancy. In this case, the surviving partner would automatically become the owner of any property so held, including real estate, automobiles, and even bank accounts.

STEPS TO CREATE A REVOCABLE LIVING TRUST

1. Make a determination that a revocable living trust fits your estate-planning needs by discussing with your lawyer and accountant. (If you haven't yet chosen the professionals you need, see Chapter 8.)

2. Decide on who will be your trustees. Usually, you would be the first trustee with one or more persons chosen as successor trustees or co-trustees. Remember, the revocable trust means you can revoke or end it at any time. After you stop being a trustee, your appointed trustee will have signified powers over your assets, so be sure you choose people you trust absolutely. If you do not have such a person, choose a trust company.

3. Have the revocable living trust document prepared by the lawyer you have selected.

4. Work with the lawyer to put your main assets in the trust. The deed to your home and other real estate will be signed over to the trust; for example, "The Smith Family Trust." (Note: Placing your assets in a revocable living trust should not trigger a mortgage lender's acceleration clause or any property tax consequences, but it's wise to double check.)

5. Do not put your day-to-day personal chequing account in the trust as the cheques may not always be acceptable in everyday transactions such as shopping. Also, don't put assets that you are likely to dispose of in the trust. Excessive paperwork could be required to obtain co-trustee signatures for every transaction.

6. Do not place your life insurance in this trust.

7. RRSPs can't be placed in the trust.

8. Children's trusts also must remain outside the revocable living trust.

9. Be sure the trust has a general catch-all provision to cover all property not specifically listed in the trust; however, that general provision may or may not fully cover all future assets of the estate.

10. Be sure that you are clear in the trust document about the extent to which you wish the trust to cover expenses if you are ill, such as for life extension, medical care, nursing home, and in-home nurses.

11. Even with a trust, you must still leave a will, although it then becomes a simpler document. In addition to naming a guardian for minor children, the will disposes of all assets that do not fall under the trust.

12. When the deeds are returned from the registrar, be sure to place them in a safe location known to the executor of your

will such as a safety-deposit box or at your lawyer's office, along with one original of the revocable living trust document.

13. Discuss the revocable living trust provisions with those whom it will affect, i.e., your heirs and your co-trustees.

THE THORNY ISSUE OF TAX IN ESTATE PLANNING: SUBSTANTIAL ESTATES

Unlike your experience as the recipient of an estate, where the taxes arising on death will have been paid prior to your seeing penny one, the starting point for planning a major estate is taxes. Your plans for your loved ones could come to naught if your estate is consumed by taxes that could have been properly avoided.

"How much of my estate can I pass tax free?" One answer to this crucial question is that 100% of assets can pass tax-free to a surviving spouse.

Assume that your bequests are to individuals other than your spouse, then you will need to ensure that there are enough after-tax resources in the estate, once liquidated or turned into cash, to cover all of these bequests. If you fail to take taxes into account, you could end up short-changing someone you care about deeply.

PROTECTING YOUR CHILDREN

Wills are about more than money and taxes; they also provide protection for your minor children. Your children and your dependent parents require special thought.

If you have minor children, make guardianship arrangements and discuss them with your children. As a child, "Lene" remembers listening to a "Stella Dallas" radio episode that involved a mother's sudden death. Lene worried that her own mother would die, but she was too afraid to tell her mother. For weeks she tried to ask her parents about what would happen if they died. Her fear was that she'd have to live with an aunt she didn't like. Children often think much more about their parents' death than parents realize, so it is essential to make plans and communicate them to your children.

You'll need to reach agreement on the choice of guardian with your spouse (or former spouse), and both your individual wills should reflect such agreement. The physical guardian of your children — for example, your sister — needn't be the same as the legal or financial guardian — for example, your lawyer. In fact, if necessary, you can provide all three. You might have a loving sister who would make a good parent, a family lawyer who would serve as the best overall custodian of legal questions that might arise, and a financially capable friend whom you would trust to protect your children's financial future by ensuring that your assets were kept intact for them.

Take time to sit down with your children and discuss your plans. Express that while you expect to be around for a long time, the reality is that no one knows exactly just how long his or her life will be. If possible, empower your children by allowing them to assist in the arrangements you make, especially for physical custody.

If you are a single parent with a living former spouse who is the natural or adoptive parent of your children, the law generally assumes that the other parent will become the children's guardian. If you have concerns that the finances would not be properly handled, you can still separate the financial arrangements and appoint a trustee for the money in your estate, leaving your former spouse with only physical custody. In marriages where money was an issue, this plan will provide you with peace of mind regarding your children's future welfare.

Be sure to discuss your plans fully with a potential guardian. Don't appoint someone as a guardian unless he or she expressly agrees — and keep in mind that a guardian should be appropriately compensated for these often formidable duties. Then, to be sure your wishes are followed, include the details concerning guardianship in your will or living trust document.

Failing to appoint a guardian can lead to protracted and costly litigation with various relatives and even friends laying claim to parenting your children. Even when motivated by the best of intentions, the effect on the children can be devastating.

The same set of concerns holds true if you have aging parents who count on you for all or part of their support. In this instance, you might wish to leave the money in trust for them or arrange for a financial custodian to provide for them and preserve the funds.

A SPECIAL WORD ON ADOPTION

If you have adopted children be sure to specifically include them in the language of your will. Because of historical rules that trace back blood lines our own laws fail to deal with adopted children.

In one case, a childless beneficiary of a trust adopted a child. The trust language chosen ("issue of my body" rather than "natural and adopted children") would cause the remainder of the trust to go not to the adopted child but to a blood relative of the deceased.

People sometimes use this type of language to control or discourage alternative lifestyles. Be sure to protect your own adopted children and grandchildren. Nothing could be more devastating to these children than to learn that, after your death they are not treated as full family members.

OMITTING GROWN CHILDREN FROM YOUR ESTATE

The sanctity of family is sufficiently strong that the law looks with disfavour on the disinheritance of children. Between generations, the reasonable expectation exists that family money, property, and personal mementos will be passed from one generation to the next. The law presumes that children will inherit equally from their parents.

But there are many real-world examples where that expectation is not met. Children may have their own resources. One child may be better off and not need the money. Children may have so disappointed their parents that those parents wish to see their own hard-earned money kept from wasteful or spendthrift children. Or, parents may feel that inheriting too much wealth is not appropriate for their children, preferring instead to encourage their offspring to make their own way in the world. Many wealthy people may prefer to put their estate to work directly for the benefit of the community and society. In fact, business publications recently have explored the topic of providing only modest inheritances for the "children's own good."

If you decide to omit a child for any reason, you should discuss your thinking openly and completely with your family. Since love and money are often confused in families, be sure that your reasons for decisions are clearly communicated to your children.

PLANNING FOR SINGLES AND THOSE WITH ALTERNATIVE LIFESTYLES

Much of estate-planning advice centres on married couples. Tax law provides breaks for married persons, which may not cover situations involving single persons or people who have chosen to live together without marrying. But the new social reality is that many unmarried couples may want to ensure that their wishes are respected in their estate plans.

Putting property in both names or in a revocable living trust can protect this commitment. Either joint tenancy or a revocable living trust can protect the surviving partner. However, property passed through joint tenancy or placed in a revocable trust is still considered part of the estate for tax purposes, so taxes on death cannot be avoided through this arrangement.

Also, in the case of unmarried persons with children, these children are illegitimate in law. In some provinces, however, their rights to their parents' property are legally recognized. However, by preparing a will or trust that makes intentions clear, such children can be protected.

Finally, for single people who may not have close friends or relatives to represent them (or who might not legally have the right to do so), a will and a *durable power of attorney* for health-care decisions are musts.

USING INSURANCE TO AUGMENT YOUR ESTATE

You may wonder whether you have sufficient resources to take care of your dependants were you to die today.

"Insurance is the universal estate builder," according to one estate-planning book. Maybe. Certainly a variety of messages from advertising and print media suggest that if we fail to buy insurance we will be remiss.

Let's look at the issue from the perspective of providing for dependants.

PROVIDING FOR DEPENDANTS

In a family where one or more breadwinners contribute to the income of the family, each of those breadwinners should be insured to replace their salaries. Insurance is the instant replacement of a lifetime of savings for those with dependants. However, the price you pay for that peace of mind can be exorbitant when compared with the income you could make on money similarly invested assumed you live to your full actuarial life expectancy.

To figure the face amount of insurance, you'll need to establish certain parameters:

- The duration for which you want to provide funds.
- The cost of premiums required annually.
- Other resources that can be used to meet this same need.

Since cash flow is always a concern, those with young children need to figure the number of years they have to cover until their children can take care of themselves. Sit down and carefully assess the impact of your death. Include the cost of the funeral (which averages $5,000 nationally), the cost of replacing your services (cooking, driving, child care), as well as the need to replace your annual income.

Next, decide how many years of income you want to replace. If you are a married breadwinner, provide enough time for your family to adjust and reorganize financially. The industry starting point is usually five years with the assumption that the surviving spouse's earnings will grow over time while budget adjustments are made. On the other hand, if you are a single parent, you'll need enough insurance to provide for your children, including their educational expenses, until they can become self-supporting.

Let's use the five-year example. There are two methods of determining how much insurance you need. One method assumes that the family would want to keep their inherited capital intact. Therefore, you project an annual interest rate, say 10% for ease of calculation, then figure the principal adequate to indefinitely generate interest earnings equal to the annual need. For example, to provide $30,000 a year, with the 10% yield assumption, you would need a combination of insurance and other liquid assets with a face amount of $300,000 (try not to count your family home — being forced to move on top of your death would be truly traumatic). Assuming no other large liquid assets, the cost of insurance might be prohibitive for a young single parent.

The second method of calculating insurance needs may be more reasonable. Assume that within a given period (e.g., five years), the fund would be exhausted. Work backwards, calculating the interest you would earn on the principal in the meantime and discount, or reduce, the face amount to reflect any interest earned. Thus, if you wanted to achieve $30,000 a year for a limited period, say five years at 10% interest, you'd need insurance proceeds and assets with a face amount totalling about $90,000.

Now, using Table 9-1, think about the projected needs for your family to arrive at a reasonable amount of insurance coverage.

Table 9-1 Estimating Your Insurance Needs

---

1. How many years do you want to provide for your family?   _____

2. How much will they need per year?   _____

3. Multiply line 1 by line 2.   _____

4. How much will you set aside for burial costs?   _____

5. What are your projected probate or trust expenses?   _____

6. Add lines 3, 4 and 5.   _____

7. What are your total current assets, not counting your home, less your liabilities?   _____

8. Subtract line 7 from line 6.   _____

   The amount in line 8 is the face value of the life insurance policy you need now to provide for your dependants and keep your other assets intact. This chart asssumes no inflation and that the insurance proceeds will be exhausted at the end of the term.

TERMINAL TAX RETURN OF A DECEASED PERSON

Under your own estate plan, your executor will be responsible for filing a terminal income tax return to take into account any taxable income earned in the year of death plus capital gains arising on death because of the deemed realization of appreciated assets at date of death.

On the other hand, as an heir, your income tax return will not reflect the estate proceeds, since they have already been taxed to the estate.

OTHER CRITICAL DOCUMENTS AND ESTATE-PLANNING CONSIDERATIONS

Aside from normal tax and estate-planning considerations, there will be particular matters also to be completed. Durable powers of attorney, living wills, and burial instructions prepare you and your family to cover all contingencies.

DURABLE POWER OF ATTORNEY

The durable power of attorney allows your loved ones or your lawyer to carry on for you when you are not in a position to help yourself.

Whereas the living will deals with preserving or letting go of your body, the durable power of attorney for business purposes deals with the mental and physical capacity to take care of your financial and legal affairs.

Properly drawn, the durable power allows people chosen by you to take over for you if you are temporarily or permanently incapacitated. Unlike *conservatorship*, which requires a court order for someone to step in and help you, the durable power of attorney has flexibility.

The durable power of attorney for health care enables you to delegate to a specific person the power to make decisions about your medical treatment during your incapacity, which can include the decision to terminate life support. Because of the complexity of the legal, ethical, and medical issues involved in this area, it is important that your durable power of attorney be made in strict accordance with your local laws. Medical professionals are usually willing to work with attorneys-in-fact, but want to protect themselves against potential litigation in this highly sensitive area.

Durable powers of attorney set up in separate documents are typically outside a will or trust, and are governed by the relevant provincial laws.

THE LIVING WILL

Some provinces allow a living will that directs your doctors regarding the extension of your life by extraordinary measures. This enables you to leave clearly written information on your views about preserving your own life in the face of lingering illness. Like the durable power of attorney, the living will must strictly comply with provincial law. Unlike the durable power of attorney, the living will can be used only by your physician in extremely limited circumstances.

Be sure to indicate your wishes about artificial life support for extended periods, organ donations, and autopsies. Be as explicit as you can. These decisions often involve heavy costs, so your loved ones could find themselves facing a "my money for your life" choice. Under life and death pressure, few of us would say regarding a loved one, "Don't spend the money." Your guidance, planned in advance, will help your significant others tremendously.

BURIAL INSTRUCTIONS

If you don't wish to donate your body to medical science, you will be concerned to know the burial costs and customs of your area, but don't assume that you'll die where you live now. For example, as an heir, you may have discovered that your parent purchased a "pre-need funeral arrangement" linked to the services of a particular funeral establishment. If a person dies in a different location from the funeral home, these policies are often not worth their price since the cost of flying the body back might exceed the cost of the burial. Current policies should include airfare for the coffin.

In planning your own funeral, remember to specify the following items:

1. The type of service you want.
2. The type of burial or cremation.
3. If burial, the type and general expense level of the casket.
4. The location where you wish to be buried.
5. Any other communication that is important to you.

Obviously, in order to think these issues through you'll need to do some research. If getting caught up in plot purchasing turns you off, then talk with your extended family. If you are an urban resident in a major city, plots can be prohibitively expensive, and if bought under burial pressure, difficult to choose. Better: see if members of your family are buried in locations outside the city where an extra grave can be added. (The cost of flying a body and casket runs about the same as a coach fare.) This solution may be preferable to paying a high price for an urban plot.

Once the body is at the funeral home, comparison shopping is emotionally draining. Unless you are willing to move the body to a less expensive home, you are at the mercy of the choice you have hastily made.

As a twenty-five-year-old you might be able to ignore issues such as whether you have burial insurance and where you would wish to be buried. By middle age, especially after your parents are aging or deceased, it's incumbent upon you to make these decisions so that the burden does not fall on others. It's not easy to contemplate one's own death in such detail; however, the alternative is to leave the chore for others to deal with at a most difficult time.

PRESERVING YOUR PAPER

Once having taken the time and effort to prepare an estate plan, people often stumble over the implementation practicalities. Details such as where to put each document can be critical, but sometimes professionals stop short of providing this all-important advice.

Will

You should have only one original will, but keep copies of your will in at least three locations: with your lawyer, in your safety-deposit box, and with a close relative or at your home. If you don't want to leave an original outside of the safekeeping of a bank or law office, be sure to have a photocopy available. Opening a safety-deposit box may involve legal steps that can consume valuable time if your executor and others who need to know are not aware of your wishes.

Revocable Living Trust

This document should be kept in the same locations as the will. You will also have deeds for property belonging to the trust that should be kept with the original trust document.

Living Will

Put this document on file at your family or primary-care physician's office. Place another copy with other key documents and keep them together in a marked envelope in your home. Share a copy of this document with close family members as well. If you have verbally reinforced your wishes, it will help them to implement your wishes if the need arises. In addition, file an original with your family lawyer.

Durable Power of Attorney

An original of this document should be on file with your family lawyer as well as with a key family member or the person who would exercise the power. Of course, you must trust the person you have selected not to be overreaching in choosing when to activate the power. However, if you only place the document in a safety deposit box, a court order would probably be required to open the box, defeating the purpose of the durable power of attorney, which is to avoid going to court when and if you are incapacitated.

Burial Instructions

Leave your instructions with regard to your body where they can be readily accessible to your executor. Include information about the location of your will with these instructions. Remember, the funeral instructions will be needed first so that arrangements can be made immediately. It's best to locate a copy in your home and place back-up copies with a religious official, a trusted friend, and even your doctor. A master copy should also be left with your lawyer and in your safety-deposit box. But remember, either a death certificate and/or a court order is ordinarily required to open the safety-deposit box, even if you have made an heir a signatory, because such boxes may be frozen upon the death of the box renter. (In areas where word of mouth doesn't routinely spread the news of the death, heirs can get into safety-deposit boxes if they are signatories, but don't count on it.) Such an act, if discovered after the fact, could cause problems with the other heirs or government agencies if the possibility that the box contained cash or other valuables, which were removed, exists.

THE HUMAN SIDE OF ESTATE PLANNING

Estate planning is difficult. Even without technicalities, the thought of planning for your own death is uncomfortable. Add to that the reality that the tax system is extremely difficult to comprehend, much less master.

Far too many people do not adequately plan their estates, because of the complexities. The burden then falls upon their friends and family, who are already facing a difficult time, and who may not emotionally or legally be able to handle estate matters. By reading and understanding this chapter, you have taken an important step in responsibly managing your own estate.

Before we leave this topic, we must remind you not to forget the human side of estate planning. For all the loopholes, contortions, and configurations available, the bottom line is that in dealing with your estate, you are attempting to place your affairs in order as a way to bring closure to the material aspects of your life. But do not neglect the importance of spiritual closure in the midst of all the money management. Despite the allure of tax savings and trust creation, your primary concerns should always be your family, your friends, and your soul.

EXERCISING CONTROL

Whether dealing with its disposition at your death or its use during your life, the flow of capital from a major estate could have a significant impact on your family and the world around you. Because of this potential impact, you need to exercise control in your planning. Family conflicts left unresolved or even created by a poor estate plan are magnified in proportion to the size of the estate. Similarly, the tax consequences of an improperly conceived estate plan are magnified for major estates, so professional advice should always be sought. Regardless of your chosen beneficiaries, the conveyance of a major estate provides an opportunity for the future with your gift from the past.

10

MINIMIZING TAXES ON DEATH

WE KNOW THAT WITHOUT PROPER planning, a significant part of one's estate on death could go to the government in taxes and probate costs as well as in professional fees, before the intended heirs get anything. Even if you deem the government a worthy beneficiary of your assets, surely your capital would be put to more effective use in a properly constituted charitable trust?

But to die wealthy could mean that your heirs live poor. If taxes are to be truly minimized on death, then active consideration should be given in the estate planner's lifetime to transfers of ownership of growth assets to the intended heirs or to be held in trust for such heirs as part of a gifting program under a comprehensive estate plan. However good intentions are not enough, the law also imposes responsibilities for the surviving spouse and for dependent children. So awareness of the interaction of the relevant provisions of provincial Law of Property legislation is necessary to avoid planning in a legal vacuum. Specifically there is a legal presumption that each spouse shares equally in the asset pool created during the currency of the marriage. Since the *Income Tax Act* imposes highly progressive tax rates on income, it makes good economic sense to follow the legal maxim "for richer or poorer" and make effective arrangements to split current income and future capital gains between spouses. Therefore good tax planning positively encourages each spouse to build up separate estates to provide for substantial and separate inheritances.

The estate planner's tool-kit for minimizing taxes arising on death, will include spousal trusts, irrevocable trusts and charitable trusts. In addition, there are special tax planning considerations involving family businesses and family farms to be reviewed.

ESTATE PLANNING FOR MARRIED COUPLES

100% of the estate planner's estate can be passed tax-free to the surviving spouse. In addition to or instead of receiving an outright bequest, the surviving spouse may also be willed a life interest in a spousal trust. Tax exposure only occurs when the estate passes on the death of the surviving spouse to the next generation of heirs. Therefore what is tax-free on the death of the first spouse is in effect only a tax-deferred transfer with all the implications of a ticking tax time-bomb for the expectations of the eventual heirs. So while passing an entire estate directly or by way of a spousal trust to the surviving spouse, is tax-free, it may not be the desired tax-effective solution.

Prenuptial Agreements

If you have signed a prenuptial agreement, a commonplace for the affluent couple on a second marriage, the terms should be reviewed with your estate planing team. While you can choose to be more generous than the requirements of the prenuptial agreement, you must be sure that these requirements are meticulously observed in your will to avoid potential litigation against the estate by a disgruntled spouse. For instance if your spouse is entitled to 50% of your estate and your will leaves all to your children, the family is headed for court.

Postnuptial Agreements

A person of legal capacity can make a new and valid will while alive. Postnuptial agreements between spouses who have each received independent legal advice can bind the surviving spouse to an agreement made during marriage about the disposition of marital property. Without a formal postnuptial agreement, the surviving spouse is free to deal with his/her property as he/she thinks fit, as well as challenge the provisions of the deceased spouse's will in court.

Will Contracts

Normally, a person can change his or her will until death as long as the will is validly executed. Will contracts between spouses who have each received independent legal advice can bind the surviving spouse to an agreement made during marriage about the disposition of the marital property. Without a formal will contract or a spousal trust, the surviving spouse is free to dispose of his or her property as he or she sees fit, regardless of any prior oral agreements.

IRREVOCABLE TRUSTS

An irrevocable trust is a much used estate planning device to achieve the splitting off of legal ownership of property from the beneficial use and enjoyment of the property. Ownership resides in the hands of trustees with instruction as to uses of the capital and income of the trust for the benefit of the income and capital beneficiaries. If the trustees are unsure of the particular exercise of their powers they may have to apply to the court for guidance. During his/her life the settlor of the trust usually retains under the terms of the trust deed the power of appointment of trustees (including appointing himself/herself) in order to maintain a greater or lesser degree of control over the management and operation of the trust. Frequently the settlor's motivation to go to the considerable trouble and expense of setting up the trust and then maintaining its ongoing effectiveness, is rooted in the desire to protect the beneficiary/ies from the responsibility of managing assets based on the settlor's perception that the beneficiary suffers from a handicap (legal, physical or mental) requiring temporary (e.g. in the case of a child's minority) or permanent (e.g. debilitating mental condition) trusteeship of assets.

The settlor may well wish to minimize future tax liabilities attaching to growth assets and current income flows by transferring ownership of such assets at a time when the beneficiaries are considered unready for such responsibilities. In these circumstances, the settlor can park the assets in an irrevocable trust, relying on the competencies of his/her appointed trustees to carry out his/her directions. As both the family and tax concerns can be complex and significant, competent professional advice should be obtained before and during the operation of a trust that by its very nature is irrevocable once created.

THE FAMILY BUSINESS

It is a sad commentary on human nature that statistically a family business will not survive more than a couple of generations of family control as a result of family disharmony and poor estate planning or a little of both these afflictions. Most business starts as a sole proprietorship of one owner-operator and may grow with additional owner-operators into a partnership. However inevitably once the business is truly successful with an identity of its own separate from the human founders, it will become an incorporated entity for good legal and tax considerations. At that time the shareholders will craft a comprehensive "Shareholders' Agreement" to provide for good corporate governance and the future management and ownership of the business. Most "Shareholders' Agreements" will contain a specific "share buy-sell" provision setting out the methodology of business succession including funding by way of life insurance or a sinking fund to take out the departing shareholder or the estate of a deceased shareholder. While this corporate planning recognizes the worth and value of the shares of the corporation and the role of the corporation in providing funds to shareholders, it does not and probably cannot address the particular personal and estate planning concerns of the individual.

A family business is a special situation, for it is frequently the "cash cow" providing the necessary financial support for a number of individuals each making different contributions in respect of equity and labour, but it may not be in a position to make adequate provision to take care of all needs of the living, the incapacitated or the dead. While legally the corporation is a perpetual entity with the capacity to outlive the death of a founding shareholder, the company may fail or have to be sold to meet the demands of taxes at death. Therefore the founding shareholder/s should as a matter of estate planning and business succession planning, transfer the ownership and the management of the family business whether a sole proprietorship, an interest in a partnership, or equity in a company, to the next generation of owners and managers. Since a business is a dynamic, expanding universe, planning must be flexible and responsive to change. While the will takes care of the situation of succession on death, subject to the specific provisions of an existing "Shareholders' Agreement," current planning will have identified, trained and put in place the management team and the appropriate ownership structure before the reality of death obtrudes. On the assumption that the estate planner is satisfied that the family can provide the necessary home-grown talent to manage the business (otherwise the business may have to be sold to outsiders), it will then be necessary to deal equitably with the shareholdings to reward and motivate the new generation of owner-managers and also to carve out some lesser equity participation in the family company for other family members, some of whom will not be active in the management of the business. If the family business is the family's "cash cow," then it may be necessary to "pension off" non-active family members with non-voting preferred shares to provide an annual income for a notional participation. In this context "current planning" also means affecting changes in equity participation, utilizing tax-free corporate reorganizations to freeze or partially freeze the equity of the founding shareholder by the exchange of common shares for special voting, redeemable preferred shares, so the future growth of the business is reflected in the common shares of the new generation of wealth creators.

Timing is everything and every shareholder of a "Small Business Corporation" ("SBC") needs to consider the realization as soon as possible of his/her lifetime $500,000 Capital Gains Deduction before it can be withdrawn in a future "tax reform" or simply made unavailable by reason of the increasingly onerous technical requirements of this "tax loop-hole." Certainly the founding shareholder should seek professional advice to arrange to trigger, at least for tax purposes, the necessary disposition of all/part of his/her equity in an active business whose shares are "Qualifying Small Business Corporation" shares. Of course such a disposition should also be used as part of the estate plan to transfer these shares to the next generation of "SBC" shareholders.

THE FAMILY FARM

The family farm is the holy grail of the estate planner and the ticket to immortality in the family annals. It is the ultimate tax-supported lifestyle that can be handed down and carried on in perpetuity. To qualify for this exclusive club, the estate planner, or the son/daughter of the estate planner, or the estate planner's grandchildren must be in the business of full-time farming. The trick therefore, is for the estate planner or one of his/her direct descendants to be into the business of "farming" which according to Revenue Canada, "includes tillage of the soil, livestock raising or exhibiting, maintaining of horses for racing, raising of poultry, fur farming, dairy farming, fruit farming and the keeping of bees but does not include an office or employment under a person engaged in the business of farming." Note also that "custom farming" is not accepted as "farming" by Revenue Canada. To keep the horney-handed son of the soil and the astute estate planner down on the farm with the family, the *Income Tax Act* rolls out the red carpet of tax-free intergenerational roll-overs. Every wealthy family patriarch/matriarch should jump into this granddaddy of "tax loop-holes" (perhaps after retiring from "The Family Business" as outlined in the previous paragraph) and invest full-time in the farm culture of Canada and in the "Qualified Farm Property" necessary for the carrying on of the farming business for profit.

To qualify for the 100% tax-free intergenerational roll-over of "Qualified Farm Property" (farmland, shares of a family farm corporation, an interest in a family farm partnership, or eligible capital properties such as goodwill and farm quotas) from parent to children or to grandchildren during the estate planner's lifetime by gift or by will on death, the farm business must have been owned and operated by the estate planner and/or his/her immediate family. The "Qualified Farm Property" must also pass to a "qualified heir" of the estate planner.

Even if the disposition (or deemed disposition on death) of the "Qualified Farm Property" is not covered by the tax-free intergenerational roll-over, the estate planner or his/her estate may still be able to take advantage of the $500,000 lifetime Capital Gains Deduction.

CHARITABLE TRUSTS

Once you have decided how much of your money to leave to your potential heirs, another area to consider is charitable contributions. The creation of a charitable trust should be given serious consideration if you have a major estate and do not have children or are among the 29% of wealthy Canadians who are likely to leave at least a portion of their estates outside of the "traditional" family. Charitable bequests enable you to give some part of your estate back to society. Charitable trusts may also help you to save on taxes on death since contributions to registered charities are 100% deductible from income reportable in the deceased's terminal return with a one-year carry-back for any undeducted portion otherwise the taxpayer has a 50% annual charitable deduction.

These charitable contributions enable you to reduce taxes during your lifetime and in your terminal year.

CHARITABLE DONATIONS

There are a number of techniques that enable you to give to the charity or charities of your choice without forcing you to make unacceptable financial sacrifices during your own lifetime. If this form of giving appeals to you, then you should seriously consider the various options and consult an advisor before creating the charitable trust of your choice.

The contribution can be made by an annual gift, for example, if you pay the premium on a life insurance policy on your life, that is owned by a registered charity, or make a testamentary gift of the proceeds of a life insurance policy on your life. Where a number of registered charities are to benefit from a life insurance policy on your life, you should consider setting up a trust to hold the policy for the beneficiary charities.

CREATIVE USES OF LIFE INSURANCE IN ESTATE PLANNING

If you follow the financial press, you may have read about insurance trusts or the use of insurance to protect your estate. With insurance choices, two basic questions must always be answered:

1. Can I make more money by putting my investment elsewhere?

2. Is there a particular tax advantage to choosing insurance over the alternative investment?

PROVIDING LIQUIDITY IN AN ILLIQUID ESTATE

In many estates, the major assets are not liquid or readily convertible to cash. The family home is an example of an asset that the family might not wish to sell, but if there is no cash in the estate, the executor may have no choice. In other cases, assets such as stocks are liquid, but they may have appreciated, so the estate will pay tax.

The estate may have many cash obligations, from administrative costs and probate fees to debt repayments, medical expenses, losses incurred during estate settlement, and burial costs. These costs are in addition to taxes arising on death. Even if a living trust is utilized to avoid probate, taxes and trustee fees may be owed, as well as the other cash items connected with completing the transfer of assets and these costs can eat up from 15% to 70% of an unplanned estate.

Insurance can be used to bridge the cash gap, leaving the bulk of the estate portfolio, including the family home, intact. Otherwise, such assets may have to be sold in order to pay these expenses.

To determine the amount needed for this purpose, as distinct from providing funds for dependants, you'll need to estimate the costs of the various items. Here the challenge is not to project over a period of years, but to establish what will be needed after your death to cover all of the estate's cash needs.

For example, assume Noah has an estate totalling $750,000. Let's assume that the executor's first cash need will be $38,000 for taxes on death. Assume that the provincial probate fees add another $15,000. Burial costs are $12,500; probate and administrative fees, $5,000; and his final medical expenses not covered by insurance cost $4,000. In addition, Noah's monthly docking charges for his Erikson 42 racing sloop over the nine-month period of estate settlement run to $4,500.

A total of $79,800 in cash is needed, but Noah's estate is all in land, appreciated stocks, and his yacht, none of which are liquid. Ideally, then, Noah's assets would include insurance to cover all these cash expenses.

Of course, neither you nor Noah know your final estate costs, but based upon the size of your assets now, you can estimate what cash might be needed. Periodically, you can review your position with your lawyer and accountant to be sure you have accounted for changed circumstances.

Since, as we have already seen, insurance is an expensive investment, depending upon your age, earning capacity, and insurability, you should also do alternative projections to determine whether keeping funds in liquid assets is a better choice.

But, in Noah's example, one key point has been omitted. If Noah had saved the money, instead of putting it into insurance, additional taxes on death would have been owed on the appreciated assets. With a properly structured insurance plan, these taxes are avoided.

FUNDING TAXES WITH INSURANCE

The proceeds of an insurance policy are tax-free to the recipient. However, to avoid proceeds being treated as part of the estate assets of the deceased and subject to probate, the beneficiary (or trust for the beneficiary) is specifically named as the policy owner.

11

ॐ

THE FLOW OF CAPITAL: MONEY, POWER AND SOCIETY

THE FLOW OF CAPITAL AFFECTS all of our lives. For some, capital is the stream that funds their businesses. For others, capital is the source of their salaries. For new heirs, capital represents opportunity — to assume the role of gatekeeper — controlling the flow and productive deployment of their own new found reserve of capital.

The availability of control presents your greatest challenge as a new heir. You must learn to control your capital and direct its flow, or you risk having the money control you.

Although capital can be a great source of enjoyment and entertainment, its power extends far beyond personal gratification. When properly controlled, capital can build dreams into reality. At the same time, the wealthy are often disillusioned to find that money in itself is not satisfying. When lottery winners say that they expect to keep their jobs even after winning, they are expressing that money alone does not provide for a day-to-day occupation of mind and spirit and personal lifestyle.

With capital, an individual can have a significant impact on public and personal life through investment, entrepreneurship, and charitable and political contributions. Although the modest inheritor must exercise caution when considering entering any of these potentially high-stakes endeavours, one of the pleasures, and responsibilities, of money, is to use it to accomplish the investment, social, political, and charitable goals you cherish.

SOCIALLY RESPONSIBLE INVESTING

The concept of using capital to control behaviour probably reaches back into the human genetic code. For as long as people have amassed even the smallest vestige of wealth, they have used it to influence others.

A MODERN MOVEMENT IS BORN

The development of the modern socially responsible movement grew out of the energies of the sixties. New heirs reasoned that they didn't have to give up their inheritances, to direct their investments in ways that could make a difference to society in general.

NEGATIVE SCREENS

Socially responsible investing first took hold in the financial world as a reactive screen against "sin" stocks. Negative screens prevented investment in liquor, tobacco, and gambling companies, as well as companies involved with disfavoured foreign governments. These negative screens have had varying success in making their intended social impact. A GM boycott in the United States resulted in the divestment of nuclear weapons production by that company. Most church portfolios, representing billions of dollars, won't touch tobacco or liquor, yet those industries continue to thrive. Many private investors created their own personal negative screens, often avoiding companies that have historically poor records on employment or environmental fronts.

POSITIVE SCREENS

The next and more sophisticated stage involved rewarding companies for "doing good" as well as punishing companies for "doing bad." Environmentally friendly companies, innovative health companies, and companies led by women and minorities have now become targets for investors who want their capital to be a positive force for social change.

THE 4M FORMULA FOR SOCIALLY
RESPONSIBLE INVESTING

If you plan on getting involved in socially responsible investments, you should keep two thoughts in mind. First, understand the principle that socially responsible investing is not charity. If the activity or proposed investment is not designed to turn a profit in the near future, it's not an investment. Be rigorous in your examination of any investment, and expect investments that pay social dividends to pay monetary ones as well. Second, start small.

ॐ
Modest:
If your modest inheritance is under $50,000, don't leap into socially responsible venture capital or commit funds to a start-up company that makes food containers for the Third World. Instead, explore one of the established mutual funds with stated social goals and a track record.

ॐ
Moderate:
If your inheritance is in the moderate range, ($50,000 to $250,000), you could consider "ethical" funds and perhaps $10,000 in a properly organized start-up business.

ॐ
Major:
At the major level ($250,000 to $1,000,000), while you wouldn't want to be the sole investor in a start-up venture, certainly you could afford to consider a $25,000 to $50,000 venture or growth stage business investment, recognizing that the money will be at risk and could be lost.

ॐ
Millions:
At this level, you can seriously invest in venture capital. If you are starting out, you are well advised to join other emerging investors in a socially responsible investment group.

VENTURE CAPITAL

The allure of venture capital is high, rapid returns. The risk is the loss of even more than your initial investment.

Why would anyone want to consider investing in a situation where more than the investment could be lost? Because the promise of venture capital is not limited to rapid returns. Venture capitalists are enthralled with the pace and excitement of small businesses that have the potential for rapid expansion, job creation, and societal impact.

WHAT YOU GET

In exchange for critical infusions of capital, the investor or venture capitalist expects to own from 40% to 60% of the business. Although most entrepreneurs are loathe to lose control of their hard-won business opportunities, to get the necessary capital many eventually go the venture capital route.

As an investor, you will find that venture capital presents both opportunity and risk. Any start-up or early-stage business can fail, and your exposure may not be limited to the funds you originally invest. Depending upon the covenants in the original deal, investors may find themselves involved with cash infusions and providing emergency management.

Before undertaking a venture capital investment, do your homework; in other words, do your *due diligence*.

DUE DILIGENCE

Due diligence is the process of checking to see that the business opportunity is as it has been presented in the business plan and that the legal and financial documents are in order. Since failure rates among start-ups are one in five or higher, venture capital investments require significant due diligence. The greater the proportion of your wealth you are investing, the more careful you'll want to be. Visit with the entrepreneur personally. Check out the place of business. Be sure that it meets your expectations in reality, not just on paper.

Most seasoned investors expect to place about half their bet on the individual entrepreneur. The new venture lives or dies by the dedication of the entrepreneur, so make management your first priority.

You'll also want to look to the existing and proposed capitalization. Be sure that there is enough capital for the business to continue operation until it turns a profit.

Have your lawyer look over the legal documents, including the offering memorandum and subscription agreement. Be sure that your potential loss is limited to the amount of capital you have laid on the table and does not include any "capital calls" or extra capital to be paid in.

If you don't understand the financial projections, ask your accountant if they seem reasonable under the particular circumstances. Of course, keep in mind that projections are just that — someone's optimistic hopes about what will happen, not a guaranteed outcome.

If it seems that a great deal of checking (and expense) is involved in investing in a business venture, you're right. Such activities basically are the preserve of millionaire inheritors. At that level, losing $25,000 to $100,000 would hurt, but it wouldn't be fatal to preserving one's inheritance relatively intact.

However, after you inherit, if family and friends are aware of your good fortune, you'll find yourself surrounded with numerous investment "opportunities." Just as almost everyone has one good movie script inside them just waiting to be written, almost every person stressed out or bored on their job has one good "business" just waiting to be born.

Entrepreneurship should not be discouraged, but don't cast yourself as the only cheerleader. Make sure you have experienced co-investors. They can help shoulder the burden of maintaining the business through tough times.

If you are thinking about starting your own business with your inheritance, think twice. Without adequate preparation and vision, starting a business from scratch is one of the easiest ways to lose money, next to a trip to the casino. Bottom line: Don't put more money into your own business than you would not be willing to lose in someone else's. It is better to earn the interest on your inheritance than to work in vain.

INVESTING, NOT GIVING

The underlying theme here is that socially responsible investing is investing, not charity. Studies have shown that socially responsible investments perform as well as or better than the TSE 300. In fact, many financial experts maintain that companies that incorporate humanistic values will do better than those that do not. This concept should be intuitive. Companies that are focused on the needs of their employees, their environments, and their consumers are the most likely companies to prosper in the long-run.

THE INVESTORS' CIRCLE

A U.S. group of private investors formed the Investors' Circle in 1992 for the purpose of establishing a marketplace for socially responsible venture deals. After trial and error the group set up a "deal flow," an organized process for circulating potential investments. An investors' committee looks over 200 to 300 deals forwarded, and selects 10 to 15. This process culminates in a semi-annual venture fair, with morning presentations by entrepreneurs seeking capital. The investors hear the presentations, and in the afternoon meet individually with the entrepreneurs and their teams. In the evening they share their impressions of the pros and cons of particular enterprises.

Investors then do their own due diligence, either directly or through their advisors, and make a decision whether or not to invest.

The Investors' Circle is one of several socially responsible investment groups that provide pre-screening, peer support, and potential partners for investors seriously interested in the world of venture capital.

Looking for strong socially responsible deals can take patience, but they are out there. Even though you may not be a member of an investment group generating a flow of potential deals or investment opportunities, you can locate deals and engage in a similar process for yourself.

CHARITABLE DONATIONS

Making your money count by giving it away is another route to using capital to achieve social goals.

Unlike investing, the rewards for charitable giving are personal and psychological, rather than financial. Of course, in higher tax brackets, the deduction for charitable contributions can provide tax breaks for up to 50% of income. And, as we have seen in estate planning, once fortunes reach a certain size, giving them away makes sense since taxes on death can consume 40% of appreciated gains.

But, you should still be demanding.

Set up a charitable budget for your donations, and hold the organizations you support responsible for performing their stated objectives. Watch that administrative expenses do not exceed reasonable amounts, usually meaning no more than 25% of the organization's annual budget.

POLITICAL DONATIONS

Another form of exercising your money muscle is through political donations. Remember that you can use your access to candidates seeking political office to influence positive social, economic, and political policies.

MONEY, POWER AND SOCIETY

Throughout the book, we have looked at the psychological questions and issues surrounding wealth, especially inherited wealth.

Recently, the creator of a high-tech fortune made a public presentation. A youthful participant reported what most impressed him about the presentation: in answer to a question about how much he had made, the entrepreneur said he had so much money that he had stopped counting it. The youthful questioner was so enraptured by the vision of the wealth that he did not appreciate the force that created it. The youth had given us a simple reminder that even at a young age, we allow wealth to become an end in itself. As a new heir, you must not become so enthralled with your wealth that you cannot see the power for change — in your life and in society — that it offers.

IS INHERITING GOOD?

Recently a number of groups have been formed of new heirs with the purpose of putting money to the most productive uses. Thus wealthy heirs have recognized the often debilitating side-effects that inheriting wealth can have on personal development and family functionality. These heirs have recognized that "the rich are different from you and me ..." only because they think they are.

The eternal question remains whether the preservation and pursuit of wealth enhances or detracts from achieving and maintaining a healthy society with values that promote the worth of individual achievement as well as the collective good of Society.

The answer lies either in the radical redistribution of wealth through a restructured tax system, or in educating rational human beings with financial resources about their wise and socially responsible use.

No matter what the financial situation of the family — from working class to wealthy — the control of money represents power and control by the family. In that respect, the family mirrors society. It's our job as inheritors to exercise control of our capital wisely. On a personal level, that goal translates into simpler, less consumptive lifestyles. On the societal level, the task centres on using wealth to create and maintain a positive, functioning, unified society, free of the disfunctionalities that can hold the Family and Society in thrall. Wealth will always pass through the generations. The current thinking about the inheritance boom is led by the vision that wealth is a good and transforming force for positive growth for the Family and Society as a whole.

The expressed concern about inherited wealth is that it may confer power without self-discipline. The mission of this book is to empower the new heir with a positive vision of disciplined stewardship.

The irresponsible use of an inheritance, whether it be the result of sentimentality, restrictions, temptation, or complexity, has destabilizing implications for future generations when placed in the context of the potential $1 trillion inheritance boom. Its responsible deployment, through an improved understanding of budgeting, asset allocation, estate planning, and the flow of capital, will make a positive difference for all of us.

APPENDICES

APPENDIX ONE: *ESTATE PLANNING WORKSHEET*

PERSONAL INFORMATION: An individual preparing a Will should familiarize himself or herself with the personal facts regarding the Testator, including marital status and dependants, if any.

Name: _____

Address: _____

S.I.N.: _____

Telephone: _____   Home: _____

Date of Birth: _____

Place of Birth: _____

Employer: _____

Address: _____

WILL HISTORY:
I do not currently have a Will.

MARITAL STATUS:

I am married.

Name of Spouse: _____

S.I.N.: _____

Date of Birth: _____

Business Address: _____

Previous Marriages: I have not been previously married.

CHILDREN:
I have no children.

SAFETY DEPOSIT BOX.
I currently have_____safety deposit box(es).

Name of Bank:_____

Address of Bank: _____

Key Location: _____

Status of Box: Held jointly with Spouse

VALUE OF THE ESTATE: A valuation of the estate assets is needed to determine whether tax consequences are an important consideration in the preparation of the Will. While there are no estate taxes in Canada as such, there are deemed dispositions of capital property and other tax consequences affecting various assets on death and it may become important to consider more complex estate planning techniques in the case of an estate of significant value or complexity. The manner in which assets are held (for example, "jointly" or "in one name only") is also important in determining who will receive certain property (for example, "joint" property passes outside of the estate to the "surviving" joint tenant regardless of what the Will may provide).

Detailed Listing of Assets and Liabilities of Bank Accounts (chequing, savings, GICs, etc.)

Testator Accounts Totals	$	0
Spouse's Accounts Totals	$	0
Joint Accounts Totals	$	0
Total Bank Accounts	$	0

Retirement or Pension Plans:

Testator Total	$	0
Spouse Total	$	0
Joint Total	$	0
Total Value of Retirement Benefits	$	0

Investments (Brokerage accounts, mutual funds, etc.):

Testator Total	$	0
Spouse Total	$	0
Joint Total	$	0
Total Value of Investment Accounts	$	0

Stocks:

Testator Total	$	0
Spouse Total	$	0
Joint Total	$	0
Total Value of Stocks	$	0

Bonds:

Testator Total	$	0
Spouse Total	$	0
Joint Total	$	0
Total Value of Bonds	$	0

Real Property:

Type of Real Estate	*Owner*	*Amount*
Testator Total	$	0
Spouse Total	$	0
Joint Total	$	0
Total Value of Real Estate	$	0

Life Insurance:

Testator Total	$	0
Spouse Total	$	0
Joint Total	$	0
Total Value of Life Insurance	$	0

Business Interests:

Type of Business Interest	*Owner*	*Amount*
Testator Total	$	0
Spouse Total	$	0
Joint Total	$	0
Total Business Interests	$	0

Vehicles:

Registered in the name of the Testator:

Vehicle Year, Make and Model	*Registration No:*	*Amount*

Registered in the name of the Spouse:

Vehicle Year, Make and Model	*Registration No:*	*Amount*

Registered in the name of the Testator and Spouse:

Vehicle Year, Make and Model	*Registration No:*	*Amount*
Testator Total	$	0
Spouse Total	$	0
Joint Total	$	0
Total Vehicles	$	0

Personal Property:

Description	*Owner*	*Amount*
Testator Total	$	0
Spouse Total	$	0
Joint Total	$	0
Total Personal Property	$	0

Liabilities:

Liability	*Person Liable*	*Amount*
Testator Total	$	0
Spouse Total	$	0
Joint Total	$	0
Total Liabilities	$	0

Net Assets:

	Testator	*Spouse*	*Joint*	*Totals*
Assets	$ 0	$ 0	$ 0	$ 0
Liabilities	$ 0	$ 0	$ 0	$ 0
Net Estate	$ 0	$ 0	$ 0	$ 0

DISTRIBUTION OF THE ESTATE ASSETS: The persons or organizations (beneficiaries) who will receive the assets of the estate should be identified.

First Priority:
My first priority is to provide for my Spouse.

Second Priority:
My second priority is to provide for my Children.

Bequests:
I would also like to include the following bequests:

Legacies:
I would also like to include the following legacies:
In general terms, I would like to have the assets of my estate distributed as follows: This summary assumes that the bequests and legacies noted above have already been made.
Percent Beneficiary

TRUST FOR MINOR CHILDREN: I wish to include Will provisions that will create a "trust for minor children." This trust should be included only if my spouse does not survive my death. I understand that this type of trust provides that my trustee will manage all or a portion of my assets for the benefit of my children, until each child attains an age specified by me for the outright distribution of the trust assets to that child.

The trust assets should be distributed outright to each of my children when that child reaches the age of 0 years.

TRUSTEE: A trustee is the person or entity named in a Will who has the responsibility to administer ongoing trusts by managing the trust assets and making distributions as required by the terms of the trust. Often the term "trustee" is used interchangeably with the term "executor" in a Will if the same person is fulfilling both roles.

First Choice:_____

Name: _____

Address: _____

GUARDIAN: A guardian is a person named in the Will who has the legal responsibility to take care of minor children until the children reach the age of majority, usually at 18 years. A choice of guardian in a Will is not legally binding but the Court will most frequently give effect to the Testator's wishes unless there is a compelling reason not to do so.

First Choice:_____

Name: _____

Address: _____

EXECUTOR: An Executor is the person named in the Will who has the responsibility to carry out the terms of the Will (for example, collect the deceased's assets, pay the debts, distribute the remaining assets to the beneficiaries, and administer ongoing trusts). The term "Executor" is often used interchangeably with "Trustee" when the individual takes on the administration of ongoing trusts as part of his or her responsibility in carrying out the terms of the Will. Where possible, the Testator should choose an Executor who resides in the same Province as him or her to avoid delay in the administration of the estate and the possibility that the Court might require a bond to be posted for an out-of-province Executor.

First Choice:_____

Name: _____

Address: _____

APPENDIX TWO: *WILL*

THIS IS THE LAST WILL of   , of   , in the Province of
.

Part I
Initial Matters
Revocation
   1.   I REVOKE all former Wills and Codicils.

Executors and Trustees
   2.   I APPOINT   to be the Executor and Trustee of my
Will; PROVIDED that if   should predecease me, or should my
Executor survive me but die before the trusts contained in this my Will have
terminated, or should my Executor at any time be unable to unwilling to act as
such Executor and Trustee, THEN I APPOINT   to be the Executor
and Trustee of my Will. I hereinafter refer to my Executor and Trustee whether
original or substituted as my "Trustees."

Cremation/Burial
   3.   I DIRECT that my remains be cremated.

Guardian
   4.   If my spouse should predecease me, I APPOINT   to be the guardian
of my minor children.
a. I expressly authorize my Trustees at their discretion to provide out of the
residue of my estate any financial assistance my Trustees consider advisable to
any person or persons who are acting as guardians of my minor children for the
purpose of assisting such guardian or guardians to accommodate my minor
children or for any other purpose which my Trustees deem to be in the best
interests of my minor children. This assistance may be provided in whatever
manner my Trustees in their discretion consider advisable, including by way of
loan or payment in respect of which there is no obligation for repayment. It is
my wish that the resources of my estate be made available for such guardian or
guardians so that they are not subjected to financial or physical burden by
agreeing to look after my children.

Life Insurance Declaration
   5.   I DECLARE that all insurance policies on my life shall be paid to my
spouse,   , if my spouse survives me by thirty (30) days. If my spouse
predeceases me or fails to survive me by thirty (30) days, then I DECLARE that
the proceeds shall be added to my estate to be dealt with as part of the residue of
my estate.

Tax Deferred Assets
6.   I DIRECT that my entitlement to any assets that were income tax deferred during my lifetime by virtue of them being deducted from my normal income and taxable as income in the year of my death be paid or transferred over to my spouse,   , if my spouse survives me for thirty (30) days, and for my spouse's own use absolutely, and if my spouse does not so survive me, then I DIRECT that all entitlement to any of these assets shall be dealt with as part of the residue of my estate.

Headings
7.   I DECLARE that the paragraph headings in my Will are for convenience and shall not be construed to affect the meaning of the paragraphs so headed.

Part II
Disposition of Estate
8.   I GIVE AND APPOINT all my property, including any property over which I may have a general power of appointment to my Trustees upon the following trusts:

Debts
I DIRECT my Trustees to pay out of and charge to the capital of my general estate my legally enforceable debts, funeral and testamentary expenses and all estate, inheritance and succession duties or taxes that may be payable as a result of my death.

Legacies
I DIRECT my Trustees to pay the following legacies from my estate:
a. The sum of
($0) DOLLARS to   if such person survives me.
b. The sum of
($0) DOLLARS to   if such person survives me.

Bequests
I DIRECT my Trustees to make the following bequests from my estate:
Household and Personal Goods
To transfer all articles of personal and household use or ornament belonging to me at my death to my spouse,   , if my spouse survives me for a period of thirty (30) days; PROVIDED THAT if my spouse predeceases me or survives me but dies within a period of thirty (30) days following my death, such articles shall form part of the residue of my estate.

Distribution to Spouse
To pay or transfer the residue of my estate to my spouse,
                , for my spouse's own use absolutely, if my spouse survives me for a period of thirty (30) days.

Distribution to Children

If the beneficiary or beneficiaries named above as my first priority to receive the residue of my estate, do not survive me or otherwise do not receive their allotted interest in my estate in accordance with the terms continued in my Will; to pay or transfer the residue of my estate to my children who survive me, in equal shares; PROVIDED THAT if any of my children predecease me leaving issue alive at my death, that issue shall take in equal shares per stirpes the share of residue to which my deceased child would have been entitled if he or she had survived me.

Contingent Beneficiaries

If my spouse predeceases me, or if my spouse survives me but dies within a period of thirty (30) days, to distribute the residue of my estate as follows: To pay or transfer 0.00% to my spouse's parent(s),   or the survivor of them, in equal shares, if they survive my spouse and me; and to pay or transfer the remaining 100.00% to my parent(s)   or the survivor of them, in equal shares, if they survive my spouse and me.

Part III
Administration of the Estate

   9.   TO CARRY OUT the terms of my Will, I give my Trustees the following powers:

Realization

To call in and convert into money the residue of my estate in a manner and upon the terms my Trustees think best, and, in order that the residue of my estate is converted in an advantageous manner, I give my Trustees power to postpone the conversion of any part of my estate with power to retain any part in the form in which it exists at my death (even though it may not be in a form which would constitute an investment authorized for trustees and whether or not any liability attaches to that part of my estate) until an advantageous conversion is obtainable and I declare that my Trustees are not responsible for any loss which occurs to my estate resulting from a properly considered postponement and retention of the residue of my estate.

Trust for Beneficiaries

If any person becomes entitled to any share in my estate before attaining the age of 0 years, the share of that person shall be held and kept invested by my Trustees and the income and capital or so much of the income and capital as my Trustees in their absolute discretion consider necessary or advisable shall be used for the care, maintenance and education of that person until he or she attains the age of 0 years, when the capital of that share or the amount remaining shall be paid to him or her, any income not used in any year shall be added to the capital of that share and shall be dealt with as a part of the capital.

Payments for Minors
To make any payments for any person under the age of majority to a parent or guardian of that person whose receipt of those payments shall be a sufficient discharge to my Trustees.

Distribution in Kind
To make any division of my estate or set aside or pay any share or interest, either wholly or in part of the assets of my estate at the time of the division, setting aside or payment, and my Trustees shall determine the value of my estate or any part of it for the purpose of making that division, setting aside or payment and their determination shall be binding upon all persons concerned notwithstanding that any of my Trustees may be personally interested in the division.

Investment Powers
To invest, and from time to time reinvest, assets of my estate in securities and investments inside or outside Canada, without being limited to those investments to which trustees are otherwise restricted by law.

Borrowing to Facilitate Administration
To raise money on the credit of my estate, either without security or by mortgage or charge, on any part of my estate, for the purpose of facilitating the administration of my estate.

Real Property
If at any time and for so long as any real or leasehold property forms part of my estate, I give my Trustees full power and discretion to sell, mortgage, lease without being limited as to term, exchange, give options on or otherwise dispose of or deal with any real estate held by my Trustees and to repair, alter, improve, add to or remove any buildings thereon, and generally to manage that real estate.

Claims
To release, forgive, compromise, settle or waive any claim or debt which may be owing to me or by me at my death.

Direction to Distribute Estate on Timely Basis
I direct that my Trustee administer my estate and distribute my estate to my beneficiaries as quickly as possible and, wherever possible, to make an interim distribution if a final distribution is being delayed for any reason.

Businesses and Corporations
To carry on any corporate enterprise or business to the full extent permitted by law, including all limited liability corporations controlled by me, and any partnerships or proprietorships carried on by me at the time of my death, during such period or periods as they shall think fit and to join in or take any action with any business and corporate investments or to exercise any rights, powers

and privileges which at any time may exist or arise in connection with any such investments to the same extent and as fully as I could do if I were alive and the sole owner of such investments.

Employment of Agents
Instead of acting personally, to employ and pay any other person or persons including a corporation to transact any business or to do any act of any nature in relation to my Will and the trusts contained in my Will, including the receipt and payment of money, without being liable for any loss incurred thereby. And I authorize and empower my Trustees to appoint from time to time upon any terms they think fit any person or persons including a corporation, for the purpose of exercising any of the trusts or powers expressly or impliedly given to my Trustees with respect to any property belonging to me.

Tax Elections and Determinations
To make or not to make any election, determination or designation pursuant to any taxing statute including the *"Income Tax Act"* and the *"Excise Tax Act"* which they deem to be in the best interests of my estate and the beneficiaries of my estate.

Charitable Receipts
I declare that any receipt given by the treasurer or other official of each organization benefiting under the terms of this my Will shall be a sufficient discharge to my Trustees.
In witness whereof I have to this my last Will and Testament, written upon this and the   preceding pages of paper, subscribed my name this   day of   ,   . SIGNED by the Testator,   , in our presence and attested to by us in the Testator's presence and in the presence of each other.

Witness

Name: _____

Address: _____

Occupation: _____

Witness

Name: _____

Address: _____

Occupation: _____

AFFIDAVIT OF EXECUTION

CANADA

PROVINCE of

TO WIT:

I,   , of   , in the Province of   , MAKE OATH AND SAY:

   1.   I am one of the subscribing witnesses to the Last Will of the testator,

.

   2.   The Will is dated the   day of   , and is marked as Exhibit A to this Affidavit.

   3.   When the testator signed the Will, I believe the testator

3.1   was 18 years of age or more

3.2   understood that the document being signed was the testator's Last Will

3.3   was competent to sign the Will.

   4.   The testator, myself, and the other witness to the Will,   ,
were all present together when the witnesses and the testator signed the Will.

( ) **5.**   That no interlineations, alterations, erasures, or obliterations were made to the Will before the testator and the witnesses signed the Will.

- OR -

( ) **5.**   That the following interlineations, alterations, erasures, or obliterations were made to the Will before the testator and the witnesses signed the Will.

Witness

   SWORN BEFORE ME

   AFFIRMED BEFORE ME

in   , in the Province of   , this   day of   , .

         Commissioner for Oaths

         Notary Public

in and for the Province of

(My Commission expires:)

APPENDIX THREE: *LIVING WILL*

TO MY FAMILY, PHYSICIAN AND ALL OTHERS CONCERNED:

I,   , being of sound mind, wilfully and voluntarily, direct that if the time comes when I can no longer take part in decisions for my own health care, that this statement stand as an expression of my wishes and directions.

If at such a time the situation should arise in which there is no reasonable expectation of my recovery from extreme physical or mental disability, I direct that I be allowed to die and not be kept alive by medications, artificial means or "heroic measures."

I do, however, ask that medication be mercifully administered to me to alleviate suffering even though this may shorten my remaining life.

AND for greater clarification I specifically list the following life sustaining measures either to BE undertaken or NOT be undertaken on my behalf:

YES   NO

X   Cardiopulmonary Resuscitation (CPR)

X   Ventilation (breathing machine)

X   Dialysis (kidney machine)

X   Life saving surgery

X   Blood transfusion

X   Life saving antibiotics

X   Tube feedings

Additional life sustaining measures are directed as follows:

This statement is made after careful consideration and is in accordance with my strong convictions and beliefs. I want the wishes and directions here expressed carried out to the extent permitted by law. Insofar as they are not legally enforceable, I hope that those to whom this Living Will is addressed will regard themselves as morally bound by these provisions.

DATED at   , in the Province of   , this   day of   ,   .

Witness Name _____

Witness Name _____

APPENDIX FOUR: *GENERAL POWER OF ATTORNEY — LONG*

I,   , residing at   ,   ,   , appoint residing at   ,   ,   , as my attorney in my name and to do on my behalf and for my sole benefit anything that I can lawfully do by an attorney and without limiting the generality of the foregoing, to:

1. Demand and receive from any person all sums of money, securities for money, debts, goods, chattels, effects and things which are owing, payable or belonging to me, or for the principal money and interest in respect of any mortgage or other security, or for the interest or dividends payable to me in respect of any shares, stocks, or interest which I hold in any company or for any money or securities for money which are due in respect of any bond, note, bill of exchange, balance of account, consignment, contract, decree, judgment, order or execution or upon any other account.

2. Upon the receipt of any sum of money, securities for money, debts, goods, chattels, effects or things due, owing, payable or belonging to me, my attorney may sign receipts, releases and acquittances, certificates, conveyances, surrenders, assignments, satisfaction pieces, discharges of judgments, partial discharges of judgments, discharges of liens, partial discharges of liens, discharges of mortgages, partial discharges of mortgages, assignments of mortgages without personal covenants, transfers of mortgages without personal covenants, memorials or other discharges that may be required.

3. Examine, settle, liquidate or adjust any accounts between myself and any person. Sign any cheque or order that may be required for the payment of money, bill of exchange or note in which I am interested. Draw upon any bank, trust company or person for any sum of money that is to my credit and to deposit this money in any bank, trust company or other place and at the discretion of my attorney, to withdraw this money from time to time as I could do.

4. In the case of neglect, refusal or delay on the part of any person to render true and full accounts and payments of debts due to me, to compel him or them to do so, and for that purpose to take any legal action as my attorney shall think fit; also to appear before any of the courts of law, and to sue, plead, answer, defend and reply in all matters and causes concerning the said debts; and also to exercise all powers of sale or foreclosure and all powers vested in me by any mortgage belonging to me as mortgagee; also to execute conveyances under power of sale and transfers under power of sale, and to make applications for foreclosure.

5. In case of any dispute with any person concerning any of the above matters, to submit any such dispute to arbitration as my attorney may see fit; to accept part in satisfaction for the payment of the whole of any debt or to grant an extension of time for the payment of the same, either with or without taking security, as to my attorney shall appear most expedient.

6. Take possession of and let, sell, manage and improve my real estate and to appoint any agents in managing the same, and to remove such agents, and appoint others using the same power and discretion as I might do.

7.   Sign all leases and agreements for lease as shall be required or necessary in the care and management of my property and to receive and collect all rents that may be payable to me and in my name to give effectual receipts therefor.

8.   Demand and sue for all rents and profits due in respect of my property and to use all lawful means for recovering the rents and profits and for ejecting from the said property all tenants and occupants who are in default, and for determining the tenancy or occupancy and for obtaining, recovering and retaining possession of all or any of the property held or occupied by such persons so making default.

9.   See as my attorney decides is reasonable or expedient, all mortgages and other securities for money, debts, choses in action, stocks, shares, bonds, goods, chattels and all other personal property whatsoever owned by me, and to assign or transfer the above to the purchaser, and to execute such assignments of mortgage, transfers of mortgage, assignments of agreements for sale, transfers of stock, bills of sale, conveyances, transfers and assurances with power to give credit for the whole or any part of the purchase money and to permit the purchase money to remain unpaid for whatever time and upon whatever security my attorney shall think proper.

10.   If or when my attorney decides to sell all my real estate which I own or any interest I have in any real estate, either separately or in parcels and by public auction or private contract as my attorney shall see as reasonable and expedient; my attorney shall execute all agreements for sale, including options to purchase, assignments of agreements for sale, conveyances, assurances, deeds, transfers, withdrawals of caveat and partial withdrawals of caveat, also to execute any plan of subdivision of any properties; with power in connection with the sale of any of the above property to give credit for the whole or any part of the purchase price and to permit the purchase price to remain unpaid for whatever times and upon whatever security, real or personal either including the purchased property or not as my attorney shall think proper.

11.   Mortgage and borrow money upon the security of my property, real or personal wherever situated, and in such sums and upon such terms and conditions as my attorney may see as expedient, and for such purposes to sign all mortgages or other instruments which may be required, which mortgages may contain the usual covenants and powers of sale, and such further covenants, clauses and conditions as the mortgagee may require and my attorney may deem expedient, and to give such bonds or promissory notes collateral to the mortgage as may be necessary in connection therewith and collateral thereto, and to repay the said mortgage moneys at such times as my attorney may see as expedient.

12.   Execute all deeds, assurances, covenants and things as shall be required and as my attorney shall see fit for any of the purposes above, and to sign and give receipts for any sum of money which shall come to his hands by virtue of the powers of this instrument, which receipts whether given in my name or that of my attorney shall exempt the person paying such sum of money from all responsibility of seeing to the application thereof.

13. Execute proxies or other instruments authorizing a person to attend and vote on my behalf at meetings of holders of shares, stocks, bonds, debentures and funds of companies in which I hold shares, stocks, bonds, debentures or funds.

14. Have access to examine, deposit, remove or replace any contents of any safety deposit box I may have in any institution.

I GRANT FULL POWER to my attorney to substitute and appoint one or more attorney or attorneys under my attorney with the same or more limited powers, and in my attorney's discretion to remove such attorneys.

I covenant for my heirs, executors and administrators to ratify whatever my attorney (or his/her substitute) shall do by virtue of this instrument, including whatever shall be done between the time of my death or of the revocation of this instrument, and the time my attorney (or such substitute) becomes aware of my death or the revocation of this instrument.

This power of attorney shall remain in full force until due notice in writing of its revocation shall have been given to   .

IN WITNESS WHEREOF I have executed this document on the   day of   , in   , in the Province of   .

Witness Name _____

Witness Name _____

AFFIDAVIT OF EXECUTION
CANADA
PROVINCE OF
TO WIT:

I,   , of   , in the Province of   , MAKE OATH AND SAY:

1. That I was personally present and did see   referred to in the attached General Power of Attorney, who is personally known to me to be the person named therein, duly sign and execute the same for the purpose named therein.

2. The General Power of Attorney was executed in   , in the Province of   , and I am the subscribing witness thereto.

3. That I know the Donor and the Donor is in my belief, of the full age of Nineteen (19) years.

Witness

  SWORN BEFORE ME
  AFFIRMED BEFORE ME

in   , in the Province of   , this   day of   , .
      Commissioner for Oaths
      Notary Public
in and for the Province of
(My Commission expires:)

APPENDIX FIVE: *POWER OF ATTORNEY FOR PERSONAL CARE*

(Made in accordance with the Substitute Decisions Act, 1992)

1. I,   , revoke any previous power of attorney for personal care made by me.

2. I APPOINT   to be my attorney for personal care in accordance with the Substitute Decisions Act, 1992.

3. If the person(s) I have appointed, or any one of them, cannot or will not be my attorney because of refusal, resignation, death, mental incapacity, or removal by the court, I SUBSTITUTE   to act as my attorney for personal care in the same manner and subject to the same authority as the person he or she is replacing.

I further provide that the declaration of the above named substitute attorney(s) that the original attorney(s) named in this document is or are unable to unwilling to act will be determinative of the authority of the substitute attorney(s) to act.

4. I give my attorney(s) the AUTHORITY to make any personal care decision for me that I am mentally incapable of making for myself, including the giving or refusing of consent to treatment to which the Consent Treatment Act, 1992, applies, subject to the Substitute Decisions Act, 1992, and any instructions, conditions, or restrictions contained in this form.

5. The following instructions, conditions, or restrictions apply to this power of attorney for personal care:

Further instructions, conditions, and restrictions in the form of a Living Will are attached to this power of attorney for personal care.

6. I AUTHORIZE compensation to my attorney(s) for personal care from my property in accordance with the fee scale prescribed by regulation for the compensation of guardians of property made pursuant to section 90 of the Substitute Decisions Act, 1992.

Date _____

Grantor_____

We have no reason to believe that the grantor is incapable of giving a continuing power of attorney for personal care or making decisions in respect of which instructions are contained in this power of attorney. We have signed this power of attorney in the presence of the person whose name appears above and in the presence of each other.

Date _____

Witness Name:_____

Address: _____

Date _____

Witness Name:_____

Address: _____

APPENDIX SIX: RESOURCES

The following is a list of government institutions and industry associations to call:

Government Pension Programs:
* Canada Pension Plan (CPP)
* Old Age Security (OAS)
* Guaranteed Income Supplement (GIS)
* Spouse's Allowance (SPA)
* Foreign Pensions
* Look up "Income Security Programs" in the Government of Canada section of the blue pages of all telephone directories for the office nearest you.

Revenue Canada
* Taxation
✝ Registered Pension Plans
* RRSPs, RRIFs, Annuities
* Look up "Revenue Canada" in the Government of Canada section of the blue pages of all telephone directories for the nearest district taxation office or for the automated Tax Information Phone Service (TIPS) number.
* On the cover sheet with your income tax package or at the back of your General Income Tax Guide, more current and topic specific phone numbers.

Superintendent of Financial Institutions
* Overall regulator for federally registered companies: banks, trusts, investment, and pensions plans.
* Call 1-800-385-8647

Provincial Pension Commissions
* Most company registered pension plans are regulated by the applicable provincial commission.

British Columbia	(604) 387-1002
Alberta	(403) 427-0832
Saskatchewan	(306) 787-2458
Manitoba	(204) 945-2742
Ontario	(416) 963-0522
Quebec	(418) 643-8292
New Brunswick	(506) 453-3940
Nova Scotia	(902) 424-5704
P.E.I.	(902) 368-4030
Newfoundland	(709) 576-6064

The Investment Dealers Association (IDA)
* The association that represents investment dealers, investment professionals and stock brokers.
* Call: (416) 364-6133

The Investment Funds Institute of Canada (IFIC)
* The association that represents the mutual fund industry.
* Call: (416) 363-2158

The Canadian Association of Financial Planners (CAFP)
* The association that represents financial planners.
* Call: (416) 966-9928

The Canadian Bankers' Association
* The association that represents the banking industry.
* Call: (416) 362-6092

The Trust Companies Association of Canada
* The association that represents the trust companies.
* Call: (613) 563-3205

The Canadian Life & Health Insurance Association (CLHIA)
* The association that represents the insurance industry.
* Call: 1-800-268-8099

The Canadian Institute of Chartered Accountants (CICA)
* The association that represents the provincial institutes of Chartered Accountants nationally.
* Call: (416) 977-3222

SOURCES

INTRODUCTION
Avery, Robert B., and Michael S. Rendall, "Inheritance and Wealth," Cornell University for Presentation at the Philanthropy Roundtable, November 11, 1993, "The Cornell Study."

Avery, Robert B., and Michael S. Rendall, "Estimating the Size and Distribution of Baby Boomers' Prospective Inheritances." Cornell University for Presentation at the Philanthropy Roundtable, November 11, 1993. "The Cornell Study." The bequests of $10.4 trillion by 2040 had been projected in 1989 dollars. In 1995, the dollar had already inflated by 20%, so the eventual total of the bequests possibly will vary in nominal terms, depending upon the cause of inflation.

PART 1: INHERITING THE PAST
Chapter 1. Avoiding Inheritance Pitfalls
The Christian Science Monitor, September 10, 1992, p. 8.

Domini, Amy L., with Dennis Pearne and Sharon L. Rich, *The Challenges of Wealth*. Homewood, Ill. Dow Jones-Irwin, 1988.

Fields, Rick, with Peggy Taylor, Rex Weyler, and Rick Ingrasci, *Chop Wood, Carry Water*. New York: Putnam, 1984.

Levy, John L., "Coping with Inherited Wealth," unpublished paper, 1986.

Lapham, Lewis H., *Money and Class in America*. New York: Ballantine Books, 1988.

Rand, Ayn, *The Fountainhead*. New York: Signet, 1993.

Wojahn, Ellen, "Share the Wealth, Spoil the Child?" *Inc.*, August 1989, pp. 64–77.

Chapter 2. Family Matters
Adler, Bill, *Great Lawyer Stories*. New York: Carol Publishing Group, 1992.

Cunningham, Roger A., William B. Stoebuck, and Dale A. Whitman, *The Law of Property*, 2nd ed. St. Paul: West Publishing, 1993.

Davies, Robertson, *The Manticore*. New York: Penguin, 1976.

Dukeminier, Jesse, and Stanley M. Johanson, *Wills, Trusts and Estates*, 4th ed. Boston: Little, Brown, 1990.

Gubernick, Lisa, and Alexander Parker, "The Outsider." *Forbes*, October 26, 1987, pp. 38–42.

McGovern, William M., Jr., Sheldon F. Kurtz, and Jan Ellen Rein, *Wills, Trusts and Estates Including Taxation and Future Interests*. St. Paul: West Publishing, 1988.

Mennell, Robert L., *Wills and Trusts in a Nutshell*. St. Paul: West Publishing, 1979.

Mitchell, Margaret, *Gone with the Wind*. New York: Macmillan, 1936, p. 38.

Nash, Alanna, "The Woman Who Overturned an Empire." *Ms.*, June 1986, pp. 44–46+.

Chapter 3. Accepting the Inheritance

Black's Law Dictionary, 5th ed. St. Paul: West Publishing, 1979.

Dacey, Norman F., *How to Avoid Probate*, 5th ed. 1993.

Dukeminier, Jesse, and Stanley M. Johanson, *Wills, Trusts and Estates*, 4th ed. Boston: Little, Brown, 1990.

Dunn, Don. "First Things First: A Last Will and Testament." *Business Week*, December 9, 1991, pp. 108–109.

Hutton, Cynthia. "Keeping It in the Family," *Fortune*, Fall 1987, pp. 111–24.

Manning, Jerome A., *Estate Planning: How to Preserve Your Estate for Your Loved Ones*. New York: Practising Law Institute, 1992.

McNulty, John K. *Federal Estate and Gift Taxation in a Nutshell*, 4th ed. St. Paul: West Publishing, 1989.

Chapter 4: Benefiting From A Trust

Bittker, Boris, Lawrence Stone, and William Klein, *Federal Income Taxation*, 6th ed. Boston: Little, Brown, 1984.

Gadsden, Stephen, *The Authoritative Canadian Guide to Understanding Retirement Options*. Toronto: McGraw-Hill Ryerson, 1995.

Hutton, Cynthia, "Keeping It in the Family." *Fortune*, Fall 1987, pp. 111–24.

McGovern, William M., Jr., *Wills, Trusts and Future Interests: An Introduction to Estate Planning Cases and Materials*. St. Paul: West Publishing, 1983.

McNulty, John K., *Federal Income Taxation of Individuals in a Nutshell*, 4th ed. St. Paul: West Publishing, 1988.

Samansky, Allan J., *Charitable Contributions and Federal Taxes*. Charlottesville: Michie Company, 1993.

PART II: MAXIMIZING THE PRESENT

Chapter 5. Money Management

Bamford, Janet, Jeff Slyskal, Emily Card, and Aileen Jacobsen, *The Consumer Reports Money Book*. Yonkers: Consumers Union, 1992.

Bittker, Boris, Lawrence Stone, and William Klein, *Federal Income Taxation*, 6th ed. Boston: Little, Brown, 1984.

Card, Emily, *The Ms. Money Book*. New York: E.P. Dutton, 1990.

Gadsden, Stephen, *The Canadian Mutual Fund Handbook*. Toronto: McGraw-Hill Ryerson, 1995.

McNulty, John K., *Federal Income Taxation of Individuals*, 4th ed. St. Paul: West Publishing, 1988.

Tax Loopholes: Everything the Law Allows. New York: Boardroom Reports, 1993.

Tyson, Eric, *Personal Finance for Dummies*. San Mateo, Calif.: IDG Books, 1994.

Chapter 6. Allocating Your Assets

Card, Emily, *The Ms. Money Book*. New York: E.P. Dutton, 1990.

Evans and Archer, "Diversification and the Reduction of Dispersion: An Empirical Analysis." *Journal of Finance*, December 1968.

Gadsden, Stephen, *Investing for Life*. Toronto: McGraw-Hill Ryerson, 1997.

Perritt, Gerald, and Alan Lavine, *Diversify Your Way to Wealth*. Chicago, Probus Publishing Company, 1994.

Wall, Ginita, *The Way to Invest*. New York: Henry Holt, 1995.

Chapter 8. Advice on Advisors

Bamford, Janet, Jeff Slyskal, Emily Card, and Aileen Jacobson, *The Consumer Reports Money Book*. Yonkers: Consumers Union, 1992.

Card, Emily. "Expert Advice: What a Financial Planner Can and Can't Do for You," in *Ms.*, vol. 15, October 1986, pp. 40–43.

Card, Emily, "How to Complain." *Ms.*, September 1985, pp. 26+.

Fisher, Roger, and William Ury, *Getting to Yes: Negotiating Agreement Without Giving In*. New York: Penguin, 1981.

PART III: PROVIDING FOR THE FUTURE
Chapter 9. Planning Your Estate

Card, Emily, "Planning Your Parents' Estate." *Working Woman*, August 1992, p. 39.

Card, Emily, "Writing Your Will." *Ms.*, July 1984, pp. 88–92.

Dukeminier, Jesse, and Stanley M. Johanson, *Wills, Trusts and Estates*, 4th ed. Boston: Little, Brown, 1990.

Gamble, Richard H., "Estate Planning for the Unmarried Person," April 1986, pp. 25–28.

Hutton, Cynthia, "Keeping It in the Family." *Fortune*, Fall 1987, pp. 111–24.

Living Trusts. New York: Boardroom Classics, 1993.

Manning, Jerome A., *Estate Planning*, 4th ed. New York: Practising Law Institute, 1991.

McGovern, William M., Jr., *Wills, Trusts and Future Interests: An Introduction to Estate Planning Cases and Materials*. St. Paul: West Publishing, 1983.

McNulty, John K., *Federal Income Taxation of Individuals in a Nutshell*, 4th ed. St. Paul: West Publishing, 1988.

Mooney, F. Bentley, Jr., *Preserving Your Wealth*. Chicago: Probus, 1993.

Peat, W. Leslie, and Stephanie J. Willbanks, *Federal Estate and Gift Taxation: An Analysis and Critique*. St. Paul: West Publishing, 1991.

Samansky, Allan J., *Charitable Contributions and Federal Taxes*. Charlottesville: Michie Company, 1993.

Schwartzberg, Harold, and Jule E. Stocker, *Stocker on Drawing Wills*, 10th ed. New York: Practising Law Institute, 1987.

Ibid., 1990 Supplement.

Tax Loopholes: Everything the Law Allows. New York: Boardroom Reports, 1993.

Gottlieb, Carrie, and Richard I. Kirkland, Jr., "Should You Leave It All to the Children?", *Fortune*, September 29, 1986, pp. 18–26.

Gamble, Richard H., "Estate Planning for the Unmarried Person." *Trusts and Estates*, April 1986, pp. 25–28.

Chapter 10. Minimizing Taxes on Death

American Demographics, vol. 15, no. 5, May 1992, pp. 46–49.

Card, Emily. "Yours, Mine and Ours," in *Ms.*, TK

Condon, Gerald, and Jeffrey Condon. *Beyond the Grave*. New York: Harper Business, 1995.

Dukeminier, Jesse, and Stanley M. Johanson, *Wills, Trusts and Estates*, 4th ed. Boston: Little, Brown, 1990.

First, David M., "Wills: Importance of Tax Apportionment Clauses." *CPA Journal*, April 1989, pp. 71–72.

The Guide to Gifts and Bequests, 1995—1997. New York: The Institutions Press, 1995.

Hunt, James, Life Insurance Actuary, Board of Consumer Federation of America, Insurance Group, interview.

Hutton, Cynthia, "Keeping It in the Family," *Fortune*, Fall 1987, pp. 111–24.

Living Trusts. New York: Boardroom Classics, 1993.

Manning, Jerome A., *Estate Planning: How to Preserve Your Estate for Your Loved Ones*. New York: Practising Law Institute, 1992.

McGovern, William M., Jr., *Wills, Trusts and Future Interests: An Introduction to Estate Planning Cases and Materials*. St. Paul: West Publishing, 1983.

McGovern, John K., *Federal Income Taxation of Individuals in a Nutshell*, 4th ed. St. Paul: West Publishing, 1988.

Peat, W. Leslie, and Stephanie J. Willbanks, *Federal Estate and Gift Taxation: An Analysis and Critique*. St. Paul: West Publishing, 1991.

Planning Your Estate. Berkeley: Nolo Press, 1994.

Samansky, Allan J., *Charitable Contributions and Federal Taxes*. Charlottesville: Michie Company, 1993.

Schwartzberg, Harold, and Jule E. Stocker, *Stocker on Drawing Wills*, 10th ed. New York: Practising Law Institute, 1987.

Ibid., 1990 Supplement.

Tax Loopholes: Everything the Law Allows. New York: Boardroom Reports, 1993.

Tax Management Institute Journal, INFO TK.

Ware, Robert C., "How to Explain the Importance of a Will." *Insurance Sales*, June 1986, pp. 35–36.

Chapter 11. The Flow of Capital: Money, Power and Society

Bavaria, Joan, "Insight." *Investing for a Better World*, September 15, 1994, p. 1.

Brecher, Jeremy, John Brown Childs, and Jill Cutler, eds., *Global Visions: Beyond the New World Order*. Boston: South End Press, 1993.

Luch, Crhistopher, and Nancy Pilotte, "Domini Social Index Performance." *Barra Newsletter* #145. November/December, 1992.

Domini, Amy L., and Kinder, Peter D., *Ethical Investing: How to Make Profitable Investments without Sacrificing Your Principles*. Reading: Addison-Wesley, 1986.

Kaplan, Anne E., ed., *Giving USA 1994 Edition*. Published by AARFC Trust for Philanthropy (American Association of Fund Raising Councils).

Kaufman, Iva, and Debbie Tompkins. "Passing It On: Making A Philanthropic Plan," unpublished paper presented at the Ms. Foundation, June 1989.

Kelly, Margery, "To Tell the Truth." *Business Ethics*, September/October 1994, pp. 6–7.

Kinder, Peter D., Steven D. Lyndenberg, and Amy L. Domini, eds., *Social Investment Almanac: A Comprehensive Guide to Socially Responsible Investing*. New York: Henry Holt, Company, 1992.

Kinder, Peter D., Steven D. Lyndenberg, and Amy L. Domini, *Investing for Good: Making Money While Being Socially Responsible*. New York: HarperBusiness, 1993.

"The Renaissance of Values." *The Green Money Journal*, vol. 3, p. 1, 13.

Schelling, Thomas C., *Micromotives and Macro Behaviour*. New York: W.W. Norton, 1978.

INDEX

STEPHEN GADSDEN

Stephen Gadsden is recognized as one of Canada's leading financial authorities on personal finance and investment. He has published 100 articles on personal financial planning, and has written and published seven books on investment theory and retirement. He has been a frequent guest on radio and television across Canada, and he has been profiled and quoted in *The Financial Post, The Toronto Star,* and *The Globe and Mail.*

Mr. Gadsden operates a financial planning practice in Greater Metropolitan Toronto, focusing on investment management, retirement and estate planning. Mr. Gadsden gives seminars and workshops to associations, companies, government, and special interest groups across the country. He lives with his wife and children in Aurora, Ontario. He can be reached directly at 1-800-591-7568 or by e-mail at Gadsden@yesic.com. Be sure to visit Mr. Gadsden on the Internet for the latest financial advice and upcoming financial planning seminars in your area (http://www.investcanada.com).

Other Books by Stephen Gadsden

Canadian Guide to Investing for Life
ISBN 0-07-552820-7 $19.99

The Canadian Mutual Funds Handbook
ISBN 0-07-552663-8 $18.99

PHILIP GATES

Philip Gates, M.A. (Hons.) Jurisprudence, Chartered Accountant, is a tax consultant with a special interest in Estate Planning and Business Succession Planning. His practice involves working closely with a client's team of professional advisors, including C.L.U's, CH.F.C.s, lawyers, accountants and financial planners. He is an enthusiastic supporter of the "team approach" to provide practical solutions to clients' planning objectives.

As a Chartered Accountant and former tax partner of a national C.A. firm, he has been extensively involved for 20 years in professional development across Canada, including the development and presentation of tax seminars and workshops to business and professional groups. Currently an active member of the Estate Planning Council of Toronto, he has been Past President of the Edmonton Estate Planning Council and Past Chair of the Taxation Committee of the Edmonton Chamber of Commerce. He now lives with his wife and family in Aurora, Ontario.